THE

PATH OF
NO
RESISTANCE

THE

PATH OF
NO
RESISTANCE

WHY OVERCOMING IS
SIMPLER THAN YOU THINK

GARRET KRAMER

GREENLEAF
BOOK GROUP PRESS

Published by Greenleaf Book Group Press
Austin, Texas
www.gbgpress.com

Distributed by Greenleaf Book Group
For ordering information or special discounts for bulk purchases, please contact Greenleaf Book Group LLC at PO Box 91869, Austin, TX 78709, 512.891.6100.

Design and composition by Greenleaf Book Group
Jacket design by Yoori Kim

Cataloging-in-Publication data
Kramer, Garret.
   The path of no resistance : why overcoming is simpler than you think / Garret Kramer.—First edition.
      pages ; cm
   Issued also as an ebook.
   Includes bibliographical references and index.
   ISBN: 978-1-62634-117-3
   1. Resilience (Personality trait) 2. Perception. 3. Insight. 4. Contentment. I. Title.
BF698.35.R47 K73 2014
155.24   2014934266

Part of the Tree Neutral® program, which offsets the number of trees consumed in the production and printing of this book by taking proactive steps, such as planting trees in direct proportion to the number of trees used: www.treeneutral.com

Printed in the United States of America on acid-free paper
15 16 17 18 19 20 10 9 8 7 6 5 4 3 2

First Edition

TreeNeutral

For Ryan, Jackson, and Chelsea

CONTENTS

Author's Note   ix

Definition of Terms   xi

Introduction   1

1. *The Most Essential Discovery of Your Lifetime*   11

2. *A One-Way System: Inside-Out*   43

3. *Your Intuitive Guide*   79

4. *Staying in the Game*   119

5. *The Universal Rule*   159

6. *A Simple Path*   193

Afterword: Seven Inside-Out Keys to Overcoming   223

Appendix: A List of My Own Quotations   227

Acknowledgments   241

Index   243

About the Author   255

About Inner Sports   257

AUTHOR'S NOTE

This book represents my understanding about what makes human beings resilient, content, productive, and loving. It's based on my personal learning, teaching, writings, and talks. For the most part, my evidence is anecdotal. My opinions, however, are the result of years of observation and practice. I've witnessed a multitude of individual transformations, including my own, that point me in the direction you will soon learn about.

In *The Path of No Resistance*, I explore what you need to know in order to overcome anything that life throws your way. And, more important, what the implications of this knowledge mean for your ability to contribute to, and not take from, the world in which you live.

For now, here's my simple request: Set aside the current ideology about human behavior that you think is true—start fresh. Then, read this book and reflect on the possibilities that it offers. My hope is that the following words uncover a path from which new insights and inspiration will flourish. I'd like you to enjoy the trip as well.

With all my encouragement and support—let's get going!

Garret Kramer
New Vernon, New Jersey, USA

DEFINITION OF TERMS

Most of the definitions that follow are my attempt to use words to describe formless entities. They should simplify your read through this book.

A Principle: A truth.

Mind: The spiritual source of energy that powers the human brain.

Consciousness: A level of understanding and awareness that brings one's reality to life.

Thought: The creative agent that forms a person's reality moment to moment.

Insight: An answer, solution, or new thought that springs from a person's inner wisdom or intuition.

Feelings: An inborn barometer of a person's thinking; an intuitive guide.

Feeling State: Mind-set, state of mind, mood, mental state, well-being, and psychological perspective, are interchangeable words used for this term.

Inside-Out: The natural fact that a person's thinking and mood create his or her experience.

Outside-In: The illusion that a person's experience creates his or her thinking and mood.

Thought-Feeling Connection: The natural fact that human beings live in the feeling of their thinking.

Psychological Immune System: The mind's innate ability to self-correct to clarity.

Paradigm: An exceptionally clear principle-based framework.

The Path of No Resistance: Look inside—it's there.

May your past be the sound of your feet upon the ground, carry on . . .

—Jeff Bhasker, Andrew Dost, Jack Antonoff, Nate Ruess

INTRODUCTION

The Golf Channel once interviewed a ten-year-old girl who qualified for the US Amateur Championship. The host asked questions such as: What are your expectations going into the tournament? What's the best part of your game? What are your goals in golf? How do you deal with pressure at such a young age? The young golfer's response to every question was: "I don't understand what you are asking." The host, figuring that the girl was too young to comprehend his words, rephrased the questions using more basic language. Her response this time: "I understood the words, just not their connection to playing golf."

Here's a line of inquiry that you've probably never considered: What do we really see, and then experience, as we look outward? Do we experience our circumstances: the world around us, our family, our finances, our job, our friends, the weather? Or does the nature of our perceptions and experiences come from somewhere else? It goes without saying that each of us has looked at a specific circumstance in our life and experienced a low or worrisome feeling. But then we looked at the same circumstance later on, and wondered what in the world was troubling us in the first place.

So, can it truly be our circumstances that account for how we feel? Do our circumstances really need to be confronted and overcome? I realize that well-meaning friends, family members, teachers, coaches, therapists, and self-help gurus bombard us with coping mechanisms to use when it seems like life makes us feel low, but are they necessary? Do they even work? Can the world make us feel a certain way? Again, if our circumstances have the power to raise or lower our moods, wouldn't the same circumstances make us feel happy or sad *every* time we experienced them?

I told you these questions were different.

But if it's not the situation on the outside that determines the quality of our experience and level of inner peace on a moment-to-moment basis, then what is it? And why is the answer to this question so important? You're about to find out.

In my many years of consulting with athletes, coaches, parents, teachers, and business leaders, I've found that those people who understand that their experience is *not* created from the world outside (such as the young golfer I mentioned at the outset) are the ones who consistently rise above what others would define as difficult circumstances. They're the ones with an innate fortitude, who refuse to play the victim. They're the ones who sail along *the path of no resistance.*

That's the "why it's so important" part.

Now to the question of why our perceptions—and thus our experience—of the same circumstance vary. Why does my wife do something one day and it irks me, but then on another day she does the same thing and I find it endearing? Why does your boss or coach seem like a monster during one encounter, but then in the next, seem kind and compassionate? Why do you get cut off on the highway and feel angry and vulnerable, but then get cut off again and feel sorry for, or even concerned about, the other driver?

The answer to these questions—an answer that most people are missing—is this:

> *We don't live in the feeling of our circumstances.*
> *We live in the feeling of our thinking, and our*
> *thinking is always in flux.*

That's why your outlook on the situations of your life is constantly changing. If your thinking is clear, life situations look like a dream; if your thinking is cluttered, the same life situations look like a nightmare. It's that simple.

In my first book, *Stillpower*, I introduced you to a revolutionary paradigm for performance and contentment, on and off the playing field. I suggested that revving up one's mind and body, by using willpower or mental-performance techniques, only lowers one's chances for success. My message: Human beings don't just have a physical immune system; we also have a psychological one. So, if left alone during times of struggle, the mind will self-correct to consciousness. That is stillpower.

In this book, I'll dive deeper into this notion as I introduce you to some new, exciting, and hopeful insights about the mind's ability to overcome. I'll continue to use sports metaphors as well as talk about my clients, my experiences with family, and current events. I'll also disagree with a few well-known experts, and tell you about one or two who just might be on the right track. But the intention here is for you to see how essential the principles that govern faith and resolve, among other things, actually are.

If you don't know my story, let me fill you in. For most of my first twenty-five years, I was a grind-it-out-at-all-costs athlete, businessperson, and high school ice hockey coach. One day, I found myself in the midst of chronic depression. I was certain that I could fight or will my way out of it. So I labored and searched for answers. I visited therapists, read self-help books, and tried meditation, running, even antidepressants—with no salvation. All I was really doing was stepping on the gas pedal with my tires stuck in mud. I sank lower.

Then I had a surprising idea: What would happen if I simply stopped trying to feel better? What if I was resisting clarity and happiness instead of allowing them to appear? Thankfully, I decided to listen to this inner wisdom (truth be told, I was out of options at that point). I took my foot off the gas pedal, and slowly but surely, the mud started to dry. Pretty soon, I was effortlessly pulling myself out of my funk, and, as the noise in my head quieted, I embarked on a path of good fortune and wonder.

I met my mentors, Richard Carlson, George Pransky, and Keith Blevens. They introduced me to the innate principles of *mind*, *consciousness*, and *thought*, which form the foundation of my consulting practice, Inner Sports, today. While Inner Sports started out as a mental-performance and advisory company for athletes and coaches, a lot of my time in recent years has been spent giving talks to teams, organizations, and businesses. Plus, I write articles for various magazines and websites about the absolute necessity of looking to your own inner wisdom and instincts, rather than to anything external, in order to rise above what life has in store.

In reading *The Path of No Resistance*, I hope you realize what I did: By looking outside toward circumstance to excuse and remedy your feelings and/or behaviors, you're spoiling the fluent, happy, and fruitful life journey you seek. One purpose of this book, then, is to fortify this fundamental tenet:

You create your perception and experience of life from the inside-out, not the outside-in.

Nothing or nobody can make you feel something you don't think. Your thinking, and only your thinking, creates your feelings. So when you feel low, it has nothing to do with the events of your life—no matter how much it might look otherwise. What I've witnessed, over and over again, is that people with a keen sense of the thought-feeling connection consistently achieve three things in life:

- They retain inner peace.

- They excel.

- They set inspirational examples for others.

On the other hand, people who, in error, form a direct connection between their feelings and the world outside consistently feel the need to cope. They look for assistance and relief in external strategies, vices, motivational experts, or illicit behavior. These people make three inadvertent but damaging mistakes:

- They mismanage their thinking.

- They detach themselves from their own inner wisdom.

- They suppress their innate ability to overcome.

The truth is that human beings are wired to rise above anything, without resistance. Our ability to get over things is so natural that most of the time we don't even notice it.

One morning last summer, for example, I arrived at my desk and realized that it was extremely hot in my office. I felt upset that the air conditioning wasn't working. But then the phone rang, and I had e-mails to write and people to see. Before I knew it, it was 6:00 p.m. and I became aware that I was perspiring slightly—oh, right, the air conditioning was broken, wasn't it?

Something had allowed me to overcome my upset thinking, but what? I was distracted, yes, but distractions can't last indefinitely and don't always work. Why do some people seem to handle adversity and get on with life, while others seem to wallow in their problems?

The answer has to do with the extent to which a person understands how the human mind functions (the wiring I just mentioned). The mind is designed to take out old, stale, and churned-over thought—and bring in new, fresh, and uncontaminated thought. People who move gracefully through misfortune recognize that when their minds are racing, or snarled up, their perceptions are distorted. So if they try to fix a problem (ranging from small stuff such as broken air conditioning to a more acute life event such as a tragedy), they'll interfere with the mind's natural capacity to regulate to clarity. And they'll prevent new thought—and solutions—from arriving.

In brief, at times all people sweat the small stuff. Yet, for some, anxiety doesn't accumulate because they understand that fighting a wayward experience always makes matters worse. This brings us to another important lesson that I hope you'll take from this book:

Knowing that your feelings come from the inside (your thinking), and not the outside (your circumstances), is what allows your state of mind to self-correct when you are troubled.

You might not feel it right now, but, in principle, your mind is an energetic and powerful source of consciousness. It doesn't care if your thoughts are negative, despondent, insecure, judgmental, or obsessive. If you simply stay out of the way when defective thinking shows up, untarnished and free-flowing thinking will emerge. And so will your predisposition to get over anything that life has in store.

Actually, you might find it gets better than that: When you allow the self-regulating function of the mind to do its job, you uncover enduring and impactful answers. And at the same time, you demonstrate to others the might of looking within.

———

The Path of No Resistance is an amalgam of my personal stories and insights about the inborn characteristic of resilience. My role is to help you strip away heaps of outside-in programming and point you back to the inner wisdom from which living with ease is born. While there's not much you can do about the "experts" who are constantly throwing dos and don'ts your way, I believe that through the paradigm revealed in this book, you'll find a better sense of who to listen to and what information just might spark something inside.

That's my point. Virtually all self-help resources today are telling you what to do. This book isn't about another person's theories and concepts. This book is built to bring out your ability to decide for yourself.

Finally, I do have a couple of early suggestions. I found these reminders helpful as I began my own journey in the freeing direction that you'll soon learn about. First, please take your time as you read *The Path of No Resistance*. Second, as the book builds, so will your understanding. Don't fret if you're not grasping the underlying theme right away. Trust me, I get it. It's hard to fathom that both external circumstances and your own thoughts are powerless against you. Once you see it, though, I'm optimistic that your aptitude to rise above anything and everything will kick in. And regardless of what occurs on the outside, determination, honesty, and compassion will become dependable norms for you.

Like I said in the introduction of *Stillpower*, "There's nothing you must do to get the most out of playing the game (or living a giving and gratifying life). For the truth is this: You already know." In other words, answers are *not* found *outside*; they're found in innate principles that rest deep *within you*. This book is the next step in my quest to point you down a path where overcoming is as natural as breathing.

I wish you good luck.

1.

THE MOST ESSENTIAL DISCOVERY
OF YOUR LIFETIME

While driving through Vermont, I passed a flashing police sign that read: "Stay alert. There have been forty-seven deaths on Vermont highways so far in 2012." My question to you is, will this warning lead to fewer crashes or more?

In a November 2012 issue of *Sports Illustrated,* Michael Bamberger discussed mental health issues in sports in a column titled "Emotional Rescue."[1] I read it with interest. In the column, Bamberger asserts that professional athletes who are victims of panic attacks, drug addictions, and OCD "put a human face on mental health issues too often ignored." He does not, however, suggest what should be done about these issues. Nor does he talk about this alarming trend: The number of people, including athletes, who struggle with mental health issues appears to be growing every day.

---

1. Michael Bamberger, "Emotional Rescue," *Sports Illustrated,* November 26, 2012.

These struggles are the reason for *The Path of No Resistance*.

Now, before you tell me that mental health issues in athletics, and elsewhere, have always been prevalent but less publicized, consider this: Virtually every professional sports organization in the world today has mental-conditioning coaches or sports psychologists on staff. And in individual sports such as golf and tennis, athletes have the same services at their beck and call. Likewise, off the field in our high schools, bullying cases are on the rise in spite of the fact that nearly every high school in the United States now employs specialists dedicated to reining in bullying.

The question is, why?

Why, with all the self-help resources on hand today (including a self-help market oversaturated with books and videos), are these psychological issues not improving?

The answer has to do with the training and methodology of therapists, counselors, and self-help experts—not only today but throughout the history of psychology. For the most part, mental coaches and psychologists are trained to examine behavior, judge behavior, and then offer ways to fix behavior. Their methods include psychological techniques, relaxation practices, motivational tools, hypnosis, exercise, medication, positive thinking, and/or codes of conduct. All to no avail. Focusing on behavior (doing something) in order to improve behavior is simply not helping people find long-term peace of mind—much less helping them live lives of resilience, harmony, productivity, and excellence.

So what will help?

That question is at the heart of this book.

But before we plunge in, I want to tell you about the far-reaching insights of two people: William James, the man considered to be the father of modern psychology, and Sydney Banks, with whom James would have loved to work.

THE INNER WISDOM OF JAMES AND BANKS

William James published his most prominent work, *The Principles of Psychology*, in 1890. In it, he likened the confounded state of psychology to the bewildered state of physics before Galileo came along and introduced many of the scientific theories that became accepted as truth. Although most people thought that his work in psychology was groundbreaking, James considered it somewhat deficient and only exploratory because, while he knew they must exist, he hadn't discovered the *causal laws* that would allow for the prediction and influence of mental life. He claimed, "Such knowledge, realized on a grand scale, would be an achievement compared with which the control of the rest of physical nature would be relatively insignificant."[2] James even compared the importance of this future achievement to the discovery of fire.

---

2. As quoted by Dr. Keith Blevens in "About Sydney Banks," SydneyBanks.org, updated November 10, 2009, http://www.sydneybanks.org/About.html.

Simply stated, James knew that analyzing behavior and trying to change it, ultimately, would not help people. To him, finding the universal principles (the causal laws) that govern behavior was the key to changing behavior.

These principles are precisely what an ordinary man, a welder from Canada named Sydney Banks, was fortunate enough to discover over forty years ago: the principles of mind, consciousness, and thought.[3] And Syd spent a good portion of his life sharing and teaching these innate principles. As a result, thousands of people, including me, my clients, readers, and audiences, have benefited from knowing that each of us experiences a thought-created reality—not a circumstance-created reality. So the answer to an apparent mental health issue is not found in behavior specific to that issue. The answer is found in the degree to which a person understands the innocence of thought, how thoughts are brought to life by one's level of consciousness, and the inner workings of the human mind.

To Syd, as it was to James, digging into the details of psychological issues in order to help someone wasn't only irrelevant, but also detrimental. As you will see in this book, analyzing psychological issues requires thought, and thought is what creates issues.

To explain one's low feelings, then, Syd pointed people

---

3. See "Definition of Terms" at the beginning of this book for descriptions of mind, consciousness, and thought.

inward toward thought and how the mind functions, not outward toward circumstance. He found that without effort people became more peaceful, loving, and successful when they grasped that their psychological perspective was constantly changing and that this perspective determined their impressions about life. What happened in life did not determine their psychological perspective.

Syd's vision was unmistakable: to take psychology back to where it began, to the study of mind, soul, and spirit. Yet, while those of us who learned from Syd have made inroads into sharing his vision, millions of people continue to suffer at the hands of a mainstream mental health establishment that ignores and even resists these basic teachings. At the very least, two roadblocks exist today that prevent Syd's discovery from helping more people:

- For many in the field of therapy, and for many who need help, it seems too simple that a person's mental health can be explained by his or her understanding of the principles of mind, consciousness, and thought—or the connection between thinking and feelings—as opposed to delving into one's past, present circumstances, or behavior.

- It's not as commercially profitable to point people inward to the fact that the human mind is designed to default to tranquility without effort. Money is made by providing external strategies, mental techniques, motivational speeches, and supposed quick behavioral fixes that prey on the insecurities of those who are suffering. I'm not saying that self-help experts who offer these approaches are knowingly offering faulty solutions. I'm saying that since most experts themselves don't understand how the mind works, they fall victim to their own errant thinking and insecurities, just as their clients do.

The turbulent state of affairs of the world in which we live, I believe, proves that William James was dead on. Until we look to the psychological principles behind behavior, and not to behavior itself, we will continue to use therapeutic strategies that, as James said, are "relatively insignificant."

Just as James feared at the turn of the twentieth century, today people are still looking in the wrong place for psychological relief—so an excess of turmoil, strife, and conflict abounds.

BEHAVIORAL PROBLEMS: CAUSE AND EFFECT

Here's an example of how focusing on behavior plays out today. It's from the sports world, like many of my examples, but examples like this can be found in all walks of life. Because of a rash of off-the-field incidents (DWI arrests, gun usage, domestic violence, etc.) in the early 2000s, the National Football League established Player Protect, a twenty-four-hour car and security service for players to call whenever they find themselves in threatening situations. Plus, before their careers even begin, the NFL puts rookies through days of training designed to point out all the pitfalls and temptations rampant in professional sports.

But even with these behavioral programs in place, many professional football players still can't avoid trouble. Do you know why?

Before I get to the answer, here's one explanation we often hear: "Pro athletes feel entitled, invincible; they're just selfish." Indeed, many people insist that life in pro sports has the ability to make someone arrogant, egotistical, or even paranoid.

Nothing could be further from the truth. As you'll see in this book, the belief that something on the outside can somehow regulate a person on the inside is why behavioral policies exist in pro sports, and elsewhere—and why they do nothing but worsen the behaviors they're meant to guard against.

Remember the Vermont highway sign? The sign implicitly suggests that driving on a highway can lower your level of consciousness or psychological perspective. It cautions to "stay alert," if you don't want to become another victim!

The overlooked reason that this type of behavioral warning makes you *more* prone to an accident, not less, is that reading the sign introduces worrisome thoughts. And *an excess of thought is what makes people less conscious.* It's the same for behavioral policies in the NFL. They mistakenly warn players that life in the league has the ability to affect their mind-set. These policies give the players more to think about, thus lowering their consciousness and increasing the chances for poor behavior.

By contrast, Sydney Banks argued that a person's experience (driving on the highway or playing pro sports) has no ability to regulate one's psychological perspective. He maintained that it works the opposite way: A person's psychological perspective creates one's experience. So when a person's thinking and mind-set are clear, righteous behaviors follow. When they are cluttered, not so much. All human beings are subject to varying levels of mental well-being; these levels are the *cause* of our outlook on life—not the effect.

What happens when one comes to terms with this fundamental wisdom? Pretty much what Syd predicted, and exactly what happened to me many years ago: As it becomes obvious that a person's thinking and mind-set are what creates his or her turmoil—not life in the NFL or any other circumstance—it also becomes illogical to look outside for excuses or relief. Again, since human beings don't see clearly from low mental states, if we act from these states (including trying to fix ourselves), we stumble.

Consider this as we go further: Once people learn to distrust their thinking when they feel insecure, agitated, or egotistical, and once they understand that these feelings are not a cause for alarm, they will no longer seek refuge in the band-aid of delinquent behavior. This is the path of no resistance that William James and Sydney Banks envisioned. Human beings intuitively understand how to move through their own jumbled thoughts, but they will always fail if fault is placed on external events or circumstances.

PERFORMANCE AND THE PRINCIPLE OF THOUGHT

Let's now turn our attention away from behavior and in the direction that Sydney Banks knew was appropriate and true: toward thought. And by "thought," I don't mean what you think about; I mean the *principle* of thought. (I'll make this distinction a few times in this chapter.)

According to Syd, the link between the circumstances of a person's life and his or her level of failure, success, happiness, or misery is found in his or her thinking. I agree. What I've observed and grown to understand is that people who know that their sensory experiences are created via their own thinking consistently overcome and thrive. People who attribute their sensory experiences to the world around them—their clients, boss, coworkers, competitors, money, or home life—don't.

Now, at this juncture, I realize that this might seem like a broad and even unusual statement. But just for the moment, be open to what I'm about to say: All human beings form their perceptions from the inside-out. Our thoughts generate our feelings; our feelings generate our moods. If people don't see that this dynamic is always at work, they'll have little choice but to attach their emotions to their past, present, or future circumstances.

As an illustration, if a first-year medical resident dislikes her boss at the hospital, it will appear to her that she has only two alternatives: change hospitals or suffer. And why not? She believes her boss is ruining her experience at the hospital. But the moment the resident sees that her dissatisfaction is created via her own thinking, and not because of her boss, other options for her future take shape.

Here's another way to view it: Knowing that your feelings are created via your thinking, not from your circumstances, triggers your free will to perceive any troubling life situation differently—or not. So it's essential to recognize that your thinking is random, neutral, and variable.

You heard me correctly. I get that it appears as if your thinking is tied to your circumstances, but this book's contention is that your thinking—everyone's thinking—is pretty much up for grabs. Truth is, the more you grasp this aspect of the principle of thought, the less prone you'll be to connect your thinking and feelings to unmanageable life events (resulting in excellence). The less you grasp it, the more prone you'll be to insist that your thinking and feelings are connected to these events (resulting in malfunction).

That's why, upon quiet reflection, our young doctor will see that she doesn't always resent her boss. When her thinking is in knots (and her feelings and mood are low), her perception of the world around her, including her boss, suffers. Yet when her thinking is free and flowing (and her feelings and mood are high), she might not agree with her boss's decisions, but she'll appreciate his perspective nevertheless. He's not such a bad guy after all, she might say.

If you're puzzled about the principle of thought right now, no worries. These simple formulas regarding our medical resident and her boss should make some sense:

resident's boss + resident's thinking =
perception of boss

resident's boss + resident's new thinking =
different perception of boss

Now this understanding frees performers in any field. Knowing that their thinking establishes their outlook prevents people from playing victim to any outside force. The basketball player who understands the principle of thought and its connection to feelings and moods, for instance, knows better than to try to fix negative thoughts when he's preparing to take a free-throw shot and feels nervous. It's his random, neutral, and variable thinking at that moment—not the free throw—that produces the nervous feeling. So when these negative thoughts occur, the player stays on task and shoots anyway. He does not wage war with his current mind-set and sink even lower.

The solution to any performance issue or stumbling block, then, can be traced back to the paradigm I revealed earlier: People live in the feeling of their thinking, not in the feeling of their circumstances (their boss or a free throw). This means that the reason for, and the way to cure, a low mood or mind-set will never be found in the world around you. Answers will only be found from within you. Understanding the principle of thought is what allows answers to spontaneously occur.

———

As this new and surprising perspective on thought begins to roll around in your head (gently, I hope), you might find the following three thought-related reminders helpful. They'll point you away from blaming life for your struggles and direct you inward toward your natural functioning and instincts:

- You're never feeling your circumstances. You're always feeling your thinking, which, independent of your circumstances, is constantly in flux. This explains why a circumstance can look troubling one moment and okay the next.

- Negative thoughts are innocent—and powerless— unless you turn them into something that must be shunned, dealt with, or fixed.

- Just get on with it: Shoot the basketball! As we'll discuss, if you move forward in spite of your thinking, your mind-set is on its way to clearing up all by itself. Answers to whatever life has in store will then become obvious.

THE SECRET LIES IN THOUGHT

Please don't worry if this talk about the principle of thought seems a little slippery. The truth is that our thoughts are slippery little suckers. We can be humming along, enjoying life to the fullest, when suddenly we find ourselves stuck on, and brooding about, some haphazard thought. What are we supposed to do then? Try a mental technique? Launch a positive-thinking strategy? If you read *Stillpower*, you know I'm not about to suggest any direction (such as a technique or strategy) that robs you of your free will.

Instead, let me ask you this: Why do you suppose young children seldom get hung up on their thinking? They don't hold grudges, they're open and inventive, and momentary upsets are quickly replaced with marvel and joy—without doing or fixing anything. Simply put, youngsters seem to own some sort of secret to resilience, inspiration, and happiness that most adults lack.

But what is the secret? And how do we get in on the act? The secret is that children possess, and are closer to, an inherent understanding about the powerlessness of their own thinking. And while we adults have the same under-standing (you can't lose it), layers and layers of misinfor-mation over the years have covered it up without our even realizing it.

For example, when my daughter, Chelsea, was little, at times she would tell me that she hated me. I know, it sounds terrible, but Chelsea would say exactly what she was think-ing when she didn't agree with one of my opinions. If I said no to a sleepover, I was the worst father on the planet. But such unpleasant thoughts were usually short-lived. Another thought would appear in Chelsea's head and, in a flash, she'd be off in a new direction. What's interesting, though, is that Chelsea seemed to have a different relationship with her pleasant thoughts. When she chose to follow her loving or enjoyable sentiments (such as when she played imaginative games with her friends or "spaceship" with me), she lingered on that path for hours.

For you and me, the implications here are greater than meets the eye. Like Chelsea, we cannot determine the thoughts that pop into our heads. But we certainly have a say about which thoughts, and feelings, to follow. So per-haps the key to rising above any circumstance is not trying to think a specific way about it, or beating ourselves up if the content of our thinking turns negative (hating some-one). Instead, the key is seeing that all thoughts are neutral until *we* give them power.

The secret that you once knew as a young child? Your experience of life is tied directly to the fact that you think, not who or what you think about. This explains why children, more often than not, turn their back on thinking that makes them feel bad, and turn their attention toward thinking that makes them feel good. No matter what circumstance confronts them.

THE DISCONNECT

If it's so simple to recognize that children innately move in the direction of free and easy thinking, and away from overthinking, why is it that adults often do the opposite? Why, when we feel bound up or anxious, do we intentionally place thought-provoking strategies, techniques, or coping mechanisms into our own heads?

The reason is: We've been conditioned by the world outside to override our innate reflex away from overthinking. So even though our minds, like the minds of young children, don't need help to overcome low feelings, we continue to jam our heads with thought, in the name of feeling better, and end up feeling worse.

Say, for instance, you have an important job interview and you're mired in unconfident thinking: "How will I perform? I wonder what they're going to ask me. Man, I need this job so bad." As a result, your level of consciousness—awareness—is getting shaky.

But then you recall a sure-to-calm strategy that a friend once suggested: Take your agitated thoughts and replace them with relaxing thoughts and images. You give it a try, but much to your chagrin, it doesn't work right away. So you try harder, and harder still. Soon your head is overflowing with thoughts (affirmative, agitated, relaxing—whatever), and you're feeling more insecure than you did before starting this whole mind-altering experiment.

Seem familiar? Well, you're not the only one. The fact is that a mismatch exists between virtually all self-help strategies and the experience of performers, athletes, or anyone when they're at their best.

Pro golfer Martin Kaymer was at his best when he sank the winning putt for the European team at the 2012 Ryder Cup. Afterward, he was asked about what he was thinking as he addressed the ball for the final, "pressure-packed" stroke. Kaymer's response: "Absolutely nothing."

But if athletes perform best when they're in a light and free state of mind, as Kaymer divulged, why do sports psychologists and performance coaches provide mental techniques that require athletes to think? I mean, if excellence is derived from a state of *no* thought, it makes little sense to seek excellence by packing the mind *with* thought.

The human mind is far less complicated than we are led to believe. Its standard operation is one of fluency and ease. Every now and then, however, thoughts arbitrarily get stuck in our heads. And if we try to do something (anything) about these stuck thoughts, while we might experience a short-lived placebo-like spike, our level of well-being is certain to plummet. Kind of like this:

> *In ancient times, fearful thinking set in every night when the sun went down. So, from this low level of consciousness, people developed eccentric rituals (e.g., witchcraft) to help ensure that the sun would rise again. As these rituals grew more and more widespread, people's thinking became more fearful, not less. Yet once it was discovered that the earth rotates around the sun, and thus daylight was a sure bet, these rituals were abandoned. Fear was then replaced with faith.*

Our finest moments are the byproduct of pure and free-flowing thought—a level of consciousness from which we're unaware of the thinking streaming effortlessly through our heads. When you're not at this natural level of functioning, when you're stuck or afraid, it's perfectly okay. But please don't look to the intellect for answers and add more thought, and then rituals. You'll only disable your intuitive ability to overcome.

Instead, simply recall that as the sun is sure to rise, if left alone your thinking is sure to clear. It's a built-in guarantee.

WHY POSITIVE THINKING DOESN'T WORK

In effect, trying to alter our thoughts only makes matters worse. This is also true when it comes to exchanging thoughts. Trying to replace negative thoughts with positive ones doesn't get rid of negativity—it energizes it. While this strategy is pervasive in the self-help world, I believe (and hope by the end of this book you will believe it, too) that the stress on "thought exchange" shows a lack of understanding about thought. Errant thoughts are just that, thoughts. And our thoughts are naturally fleeting.

But what about living positively? Perhaps, like some motivational gurus recommend, we shouldn't worry about swapping good thoughts for bad thoughts. We should just do our best to think positively and stay in an upbeat mood, day in and day out.

What do you think? Is this a legit approach?

Not to me.

It's ironic, but noticing thoughts of any kind—negative, positive, even fantastic thoughts—is a sign that you're about to steer into trouble. Confused? Let's circle back to how Martin Kaymer's free and clear mind-set pertains to you: When you're conscious, or in "the zone" as it's often called, do positive thoughts, or any thoughts, keep repeating inside your head? I bet not.

Truth is: Getting stopped by a thought, negative or positive, lays the groundwork for any disconcerting experience.

It's never *what we think*, but *that we think* that gets us into hot water.

Not long ago, for example, I had a wonderful thought about my daughter, Chelsea—you know, the whippersnapper who told me that she hated me when she was little. She's seventeen now, and I reasoned that she was beautiful. Seems pleasant and innocent enough for a father to be thinking that way about his daughter, doesn't it?

But the minute I became cognizant of my thinking, I paused and thought again, "Hmm, if she's so beautiful, boys might start coming around the house." Which led to another thought, "I was once a teenage boy." And then, "Who do these boys think they are?" Can you relate?

Now, if I had been truly conscious, like Kaymer when he made that winning putt, my thinking would have been so natural and unencumbered that I wouldn't have noticed it. From a perspective of clarity and freedom (consciousness), I love my daughter to the moon and back; I'm swept away in the feeling—no thought required at all.

Positive thinking, therefore, doesn't work because *adding* thought doesn't work. Or, said another way: If not for thought, you'd never be stuck. So why intentionally fill your head with more of what sticks (thoughts) and hinder your level of performance and pleasure?

Besides, you can't think yourself into peace of mind, resilience, or love. For true positivity—you'll never have to work that hard.

At this stage of the game, as you continue to absorb this fresh take on thought, let's pause, recap, and assess the trepidations of trying to think a certain way. In particular, trying to think positively. Following are my nine reasons why if you believe in positive thinking, you might want to think again:

1. The thoughts that stick in your head (both positive and negative) are random and not a result of your circumstances.

2. Positive thinking implies that negative thoughts are *not* random.

3. Positive thinking energizes negative thoughts by turning something that's random into something that must be overcome.

4. There is no connection between peace of mind and positive thinking.

5. There is a direct connection between peace of mind and unnoticed thinking (a state of no thought).

6. There is no connection between performance excellence and positive thinking.

7. There is a direct connection between performance excellence and unnoticed thinking (a state of no thought).

8. Positive thinking implies that clarity of mind can be achieved by doing (manipulating or changing thought) but clarity of mind only occurs instinctively or on its own.

9. Manipulating thought (changing negative into positive) stunts your innate functioning, inner wisdom, intuition, and personal development.

THE ACUITY GAP

Obviously, to me, manipulating thought is risky business. But why are some of us more prone than others to reach for this risky external coping mechanism?

To answer, let's take our new perspective on the principle of thought and connect it to the first question I posed in the introduction of this book: What do we really see, and then experience, as we look outward? And if you're wondering what this question has to do with seeking coping mechanisms for relief—it's a lot, actually.

Although few people realize it, everyone has what I call an "acuity gap." This is the gap between your perceptions of the world, what you see, and the realization that these perceptions are created via your own thoughts. Liken your acuity gap to your level of consciousness.

The narrower your gap, the better you understand that you feel your thinking and not your circumstances—so the smoother your life will be. The wider your gap, the less you understand that you feel your thinking and not your circumstances—so the rockier your life will be. And the rockier your life, the more apt you'll be to continue to look outside of your thinking for the cause of your apparent problems.

A man in the throes of insanity, for example, possesses an infinitely wide acuity gap. He believes that every thought that pops into his head is true and the result of a precise life event. If an insane person feels anger, he assumes the reason for this exists outside of him. Thus his behavior is often reckless and almost always peculiar, since, to him, it's logical to act on every thought that occurs.

So, too, will the average person sometimes struggle. As I said, it's normal to be fooled into believing that feelings (especially low feelings) are molded by the world around us. As soon as we reach the edge of our acuity gap, however, we wake up—consciousness rises—and we realize that it's merely our own thoughts that are producing these feelings. As a result, our struggle begins to lessen.

The fact is that everyone thinks dysfunctional thoughts. On occasion, I think about what would happen if I lost my audience for my books, articles, or talks. I then become insecure and think, "If I'm feeling this way, it's probably going to happen. If it happens, I could lose my house, and my kids and wife would be so sad."

Now, it is the width of my acuity gap that determines

how long I remain embroiled in this type of thought attack. And the cool thing is, the more I appreciate that a gap exists, the narrower the gap becomes, so the less often I struggle.

More to the point, recognizing that our thoughts, and not our circumstances, create our feelings and perceptions is what allows us to see multiple possibilities in any situation—including those we initially judge problematic.

I once worked with a pro hockey player who had just been sent down to the minor leagues. When I asked how he was holding up, he replied, "When I first heard the news, I was real down. But even though I'm still not happy about it, for some reason I just know things will work out for me." Translation: This player woke up to the fact that his thoughts, and only his thoughts, were creating his outlook (the edge of his gap). If he believed that being sent down to the minors was the cause of his low feeling state, he would never have noticed an opportunity in this seemingly negative incident.

I should now mention, and we'll touch on this a few times as we continue, that recognizing your thoughts as the foundation for your feelings won't, as a rule, make you feel better on the spot. But it will prevent you from intensifying the turmoil by trying to fix or force things.

Knowing that an acuity gap exists is what allows the contaminated-thinking-out-and-unsullied-thinking-in functioning of the mind to work without interruption. Once it does, you'll find that overcoming is simpler than you think. Just ask Olympic champion Billy Mills.

INNATE RESILIENCE AND OLYMPIC EXCELLENCE

Billy Mills is a retired American runner and was the surprise winner of the gold medal in the 10K at the 1964 Tokyo Summer Olympics. When he speaks to groups today about this victory and his keys to success, Mills admits that among the many thoughts that popped in and out of his head during the race was the thought of quitting. And it wasn't just a passing thought. He had this thought on *every* single lap. That's twenty-five laps of negative thoughts during a race where he was at his best.

Not unexpectedly, many motivational or positive-thinking experts insist, even now, that Mills must not be remembering correctly. To them, at that level of competition it's simply impossible to think negatively and succeed. But Mills is resolute about his experience: Negativity was definitely prevalent throughout the gold-medal race. What Mills understood, however, was that negativity didn't present a problem, unless he tried to do something about it— because then he would be doomed to defeat.

So what does Mills's experience imply for you?

First, there is never a connection between your thinking and a current competition, or any life event. You might think about the event; you might not. Your thinking might be positive; it might not. Sure, it appears that your thoughts are linked to your life situations, but are your thoughts about identical life situations always the same? They can't be. Thought is so darn fickle that you'll be prone to all types of it (including a possible feeling of no thought or clarity) as a competition, presentation, meeting, first date, or exam draws closer.

Second, as we've discussed throughout this chapter, trying to control thought is ill-advised. As Mills experienced, the human mind is pretty much a roller coaster—your thinking is always in flux.

I once met with a Broadway actor who disagreed with my assessment of thought. She stubbornly maintained that the only reason she thought about a performance (most of the time unconfidently) was because a performance was about to take place. I asked her two easy questions: "Do you think about your performances at other times?" and "Do you ever randomly think about anything else just prior to a show?" Her answers were yes and yes, which backed my assertion that her thoughts pretty much occur by chance. In fact, moving forward, the more this actor sees her thoughts as variable, the less she'll worry about what she's thinking, the less she'll tend to her thoughts, and the less she'll think—so the better she'll perform.

But, you might ask, what about *overcoming* negativity or a lack of confidence? Can a person, like our actor, make herself or himself feel confident? Did Billy Mills really succeed without belief?

Let me begin to answer these questions with another premise I think most people are missing today:

People can fight through their lows, set out to "just have fun," repeat affirmations, or focus on the positive all day long, but they cannot ever willfully change the way they feel.

We feel our thinking—and only our thinking. If a person is randomly thinking affirmative thoughts, he or she feels that way. If a person is randomly thinking pessimistic thoughts, he or she feels that way. And that, I suppose, is the bad news.

There is good news, though: In all my years working with high-level performers across a multitude of professions, I'm certain that success is not dependent on self-assurance or conviction in the moment. I'm also certain that when you feel doubtful, there is *nothing* you need to do about it.

One of the best ice hockey players in the world today, Zach Parise of the Minnesota Wild, once scored eight goals in four games. On the morning the streak started, he experienced such a lack of confidence that he sat in my office and questioned if he even belonged in the NHL.

What did we do about his lack of confidence? We had coffee together, didn't talk about the game that night or about his mind-set, and off he went.

I know, I know. You've so often heard that in order to thrive, self-belief is paramount. But here's the thing: Since your thinking and resultant level of confidence is pretty much the roller coaster that Mills and Parise experienced, when the roller coaster hits bottom, what will it do? Correct. Like all well-oiled roller coasters, it will naturally rise back up. Provided you don't interfere with the system by trying to make yourself feel something (belief, positivity) that you really don't.

Go back to golfer Martin Kaymer again. There's no telling what he was feeling as he walked up to the final green before his Ryder Cup–clinching putt. But, for sure, if his roller coaster happened to be at the bottom (he was over-thinking) and he tried to manually fix it, the system would have stalled and he never would have found the state of "no thought" he described in his post-round interview.

A plethora of performance experts today insists that you must control your thoughts, or think properly, in order to put forth your best effort. The experiences of Billy Mills, Zach Parise, and Martin Kaymer show this is not so. All you really need to do is leave your thoughts alone. Why? Because when left alone, as we've seen, all thoughts are impotent. You're free to excel no matter when or where a negative, or even a positive, thought invades your brain.

THE IMPLICATIONS OF UNDERSTANDING THOUGHT

So far, we've examined the significance of understanding the principle of thought. Unlike many resources that would have you alter your thinking, I've used numerous examples throughout this chapter to reveal that your thinking is random, neutral, variable, and powerless to help or hurt you. Circumstances are powerless, too. Your perception of outside events is solely dependent on your thinking and mindset. And since your thinking and mind-set ebb and flow, it makes little sense to take the content of your thoughts as written in stone and requiring action.

I'm not sure if this has happened to you yet, but when people first learn that their thinking (rather than their life situations) creates their feelings, they sometimes tell me that while the process makes sense, it's also a tough one to nail down in their heads. Plus, they often wonder why the thought-feeling connection sounds familiar, even though no one has ever told them about it before. For instance, a baseball executive once said to me, "It feels so strange to hear something for the first time and already know it's true."

By the way, if by the end of the final chapter you can solve the riddle as to why we instinctively understand the source of our feelings, this book has served its purpose.

Everyone hits the bottom of the roller coaster on occasion and struggles. That's why even clients of mine who understand the variability of thought sometimes ask, "Isn't there something I can do to make the roller coaster trend upward faster?"

Here's something I've been hinting at up until now and will continue to do so: When you feel down or you're hurting, no one is forcing you to look outside and blame the circumstances of your life. There's another less demanding option available if you want to feel better: You can look to your thinking.

Do you see that you have a choice? You don't have to explain, fix, or excuse your feelings by delving into your circumstances. Rather, you can look inward, since your feelings come from thought. That's why sages throughout history have insisted that we "look within for the answers we seek."

Now, if that seems far-fetched or even spiritual, that's because it is. The bottom line of this chapter is that thought, at its root, is a spiritual principle. Our thoughts simply occur to us. We don't control their substance. And although thoughts momentarily create our reality, they are not reality. When a person arbitrarily thinks bad thoughts, his or her reality suffers; when the same person thinks good thoughts, his or her reality thrives. So if we look outward to an impermanent perception of life to explain and fix our feelings, we'll sink deeper into our troubles. But if we look inward to our thinking to explain our perceptions, like the sages suggested, answers arise and we'll move forward with ease.

To demonstrate, last year before a presentation, I suddenly found myself feeling nervous and insecure. Did these feelings come from the presentation? From my lack of sleep the night before? Could it have been that there were a lot of people watching? Or was it memories of my public-speaking professor in college who said I would never make it as a speaker? You get the idea. If I had chosen to look outward to validate my insecure feelings, I could have gone on looking forever—without any resolution or relief. Instead, I chose to look inward to the fact that my thinking at that moment had crafted my perceptions of my talk. Once I chose that course, I jumped onstage raring to go.

No doubt. It's easy to miss that our struggles come from thought and not from circumstance. It so much appears as though our environment has the strength to make us feel a certain way.

But have another look. Could that really be true? Are your feelings about the same external situation a constant, or are they constantly changing? You probably don't realize that throughout your life, you've discounted millions of distorted thoughts and perceptions and quickly felt better. You've also made many molehills into mountains and gradually felt worse.

The choice is always yours:

> Option A: *You can look outward to defend your feelings.*

> Option B: *You can look inward to the fact that you think.*

Whatever you decide, though, only option B prevents you from raising hell for yourself and those around you. Why? Because looking toward thought, and away from circumstance, allows the self-corrective power of the mind to go to work—exactly the path that William James had hoped for and that Sydney Banks laid out. (More on the self-corrective power of the mind to come.)

It is so simple, yet the implications are immense. An epidemic of misunderstanding currently exists. People keep looking outside, trying to find personal excuses for unhappiness—only to sink deeper into despair. The illusion that one person's troubles and insecurities are created by something different than those of another is what separates families, communities, and people all over the world. Thought is the missing link between all human beings. It's the *only* reason for your troubles and mine.

If mental health professionals, teachers, coaches, and parents would learn about and then teach the innocent and spiritual nature of thought, we might end pain, carnage, and suffering. We might find peace.

Perhaps this shift in consciousness will begin with you.

2.

A ONE-WAY SYSTEM: INSIDE-OUT

A psychologist was interviewed on an early morning news program about the problems facing children from acrimonious marriages. She said, "These kids tend to have sex at an earlier age; they tend to suffer depression; they tend to bully others, etc." But could that be true? Or is it possible that this psychologist is providing circumstantial excuses for the behavior of these children? If acrimonious marriages had the power to affect children negatively, wouldn't all children living in these circumstances suffer? And wouldn't those who suffer do so all the time?

Experiencing life from the inside-out. What does that mean? In chapter 1, we talked about the fallacy of using outside circumstances, an outside-in paradigm, to explain why we feel a certain way. We also examined the no-resistance path of gazing inward toward thought, an inside-out paradigm, to explain the source of our feelings and perceptions.

At this point, which paradigm I know to be true comes as no revelation. I often say that I'm more certain that inside-out is how we work than I am of my own name. If you don't see it yet, that's okay. Perhaps this interpretation from *Stillpower* might work better for you:

> *Your experience does not create your state of mind; your state of mind creates your experience.*

In other words, your state of mind, or mood, varies and your perception of life tags along for the ride. When your mood is high, your old house is a time-honored classic. When your mood is low, it's a godforsaken money pit. And while that makes sense to most people, still they often wonder, "So what? What am I supposed to do with the realization that my perceptions are created from inside of me?"

The answer to that dilemma is the premise of this chapter.

Let's start with the fact that you and I live in what many spiritual teachers call a world of form. The book you're reading right now is part of that world of form. So are your spouse, partner, parents, children, friends, pet, house, car, and even your own physical body.

Let's also start with the fact that I have a decent command of the "inside-outness" of the human experience (I suppose I'd better). Due to this command, I know that my perception of all things in my life is purely dependent on my own thinking and mind-set, even though—since I live in a world of form—it seems that my life situations have something to do with it.

Case in point: If I disagree with the behavior of one of my kids and get upset, I'm aware that my thinking is the cause. This means that if I try to fix my kid's behavior in an attempt to fix my own upset feelings, I'm looking in the wrong place. And if I act from that place, I'm sure to make everyone, including myself, feel even worse. That's not to say that I won't have a chat with my kids about their behavior. I might. But not when my mind is racing and I'm taking things personally.

Understanding that we create our perceptions from *in to out* permits us to navigate smoothly, productively, and lovingly through the world of form in which we live. Although the appearance, or illusion, that we feel our circumstances often causes confusion, knowing that it doesn't *ever* work that way (out to in) will safeguard your relationships, career, and ability to inspire, and not bully, others.

Do you know that many employers unconsciously force their belief systems on their employees, thereby stifling their employees' free will, instincts, and performance level? Reason being: Many employers overlook the fact that the system only works one way. Their perception of their employees has nothing to do with their employees, and everything to do with themselves.

It's also common to misread the source of a high level of performance as coming from external circumstance and not from within. When we do so, our achievements are often short-lived. Take the subject of weight loss. I'm sure you know someone who has struggled with this issue, or you've experienced for yourself just how difficult it is to keep excess weight off for good. Millions of people go to weight-loss centers or follow weight-loss plans and start by losing a bunch of weight, but only a handful of these people keep the pounds off in the long term. Do you know why?

The surprising truth is that weight loss is not initiated by external weight-loss strategies. It's initiated by a realization—"it's time to get my health in order"—that comes from within the person who has lost the weight. Those who don't know this (the majority of people) won't have long-term weight-loss success because they'll keep relying on, or searching for, external techniques that have no bearing on success. Those who know that weight loss initiates and sustains from within will keep looking in the direction of their own inner wisdom and insights: the path of no resistance that endures forever.

As I said, because we live in a world of form, "inside-out/outside-in" sometimes gets a little murky. So, let's dig deeper into this simple but revolutionary paradigm that has the clout to blow apart every circumstantial excuse you ever came up with. And let's put you, and not life around you, in the driver's seat.

OUTSIDE-IN 101

When my son Ryan was a junior in high school, he was required to participate in a time-management workshop. The workshop started off by having the students fill out a fifteen-question survey, which, when completed and tabulated, informed the students about their time-management acumen. My son scored extremely low. However, the teacher told him not to worry. "You are who you are," he said. "But we're going to work on goal setting, prioritization, and focus; you'll be just fine."

Whoa. My son may not have been the perfect high school student, but he did not have time-management issues. You can only imagine how thrilled I was that suddenly he thought that he might.

This is a clear-cut example of what I call "Outside-In 101." Teachers or school administrators (parents, coaches, and employers are guilty of this, too) institute some form of judgmental analysis; then they label students with the results; then the students' heads become filled with stratagems and thinking that have nothing to do with excellence, output, or, in this case, time management. It took every ounce of knowing that it was my thinking that was making me angry, and not the workshop, for me to not call the school principal and tell him what I thought about this approach to teaching.

But what *does* determine one's output, excellence, or

time-management skill? If it's not precise goals or focus, what could it be?

The answer is that people who understand the principle of thought, and its link to their feelings and perspective on life, live at higher levels of consciousness than those who don't. They're the ones who manage time—or whatever life has in store—with relative ease.

What we should be teaching in our schools and elsewhere, then, is that our life situations don't inform our senses—our thinking does.

When my son's thinking is flowing freely, he is automatically absorbed, organized, and present. When his thinking is muddled, he is inattentive, confused, and unaware. So if my son looks inward (to a momentary snag in his thinking) when he struggles with punctuality, his consciousness and competence rise. If he looks outward (to the results of a time-management survey), his consciousness and competence trend lower.

One more thing: A hidden danger of this type of outside-in labeling is that it gives those who are labeled an easy out. If my son shows up late for his next time-management workshop, does he now have a built-in excuse?

No sirree. My son perceives life from the inside-out, and he's had plenty of home schooling on that subject. He might be late from time to time, but when he is, it's only because he's looked outside to explain his temporarily rushed feelings—and that's on him.

THE ILLUSION OF PRESSURE AND EXPERIENCE

Since we live in a world of form, it's easy, and normal, for it to appear that we feel the world out there and not our thinking. (Truth be told, my son went to an outstanding high school with eager and bright teachers—and still, they usually missed it.) That's the reason I cannot overemphasize the value in knowing that the system only works from the inside-out. But because it doesn't look that way, we often fight it.

Regrettably, misinformation seems to be everywhere. How about the TV commercial that claims that if you don't have pep in your step it must be the result of a demanding job, so take 5-Hour Energy and you'll breeze right through your day? Or Internet giant Google alleging that unconventional conference rooms, cafeterias, and play areas produce more imaginative employees? Or commentators arguing during a power outage at the 2013 Super Bowl that stopping the game for forty minutes could swing momentum? Or the psychologist (mentioned in the beginning of this chapter), who has been trained to think that acrimonious marriages have the ability to affect children in damaging ways?

We even see examples of outside-in misinformation in the most horrific of circumstances. On December 14, 2012, we were confronted with the terrible news of a school shooting in Newtown, Connecticut. Many experts insisted that the students who survived would be scarred for life. It was a tragedy of epic proportions, but this circumstance cannot scar these innately resilient kids unless we keep pointing them in this erroneous outside-in direction. The more they understand that the events of that day have no power over them, the sooner these kids will heal. Human beings create perceptions of *everything* from the inside-out.

In the world of youth, high school, and college sports, the innate resilience of the young participants is constantly under siege, too. I was once asked to speak at a college football recruiting showcase. On my way to the lecture hall, I noticed a sign at a vendor booth hosted by a sports psychology firm that read, "How do you 'hack' the pressure that football brings?" The words stopped me in my tracks. Here's a sports psychology firm, designed to help young athletes, telling them that a sport has the power to make them feel pressure—and they have to *hack* that pressure. And if that wasn't enough, the firm also claimed that its strategies and techniques could fix a football player's nervous feelings. See what I mean about leading our young people down an outside-in path?

Here are two more examples of outside-in thinking: If you're a baseball fan, you've probably heard of Stephen Strasburg. He was the first pick by the Washington Nationals in the 2009 MLB draft. Most baseball experts recognized his raw talent, but they were shocked at just how quickly the Nationals organization brought him up through the minor leagues to the majors. Virtually every expert predicted that without seasoning or experience this young pitcher would get shelled in his first MLB start. Know what happened? Strasburg dominated that day, striking out fourteen.

Veteran golfer Greg Norman had won eighty professional tournaments worldwide when he entered the final round of the 1996 Masters Tournament with a whopping six-shot lead. He couldn't fail with that lead and that wealth of experience, could he? Norman lost that day by five.

Life works one way. If you're looking at anything external (surroundings, other people's opinions, number of games or tournaments played, etc.) to calculate one's faculty to excel, you're looking in the wrong place. Human beings can only create their successes and failures from within themselves. Experience, talent, and environment are always trumped by the degree to which a person sees that his or her feelings and perceptions are shaped from the inside-out.

Stephen Strasburg might have sensed pressure as he took the field for his first MLB start, but he understood that this sensation came from his own thoughts. Strasburg looked inside, his mind self-corrected, and the pressure faded. Greg Norman believed it worked from out to in; what he sensed came from the 1996 Masters. He didn't self-correct. Look no further.

THE PASSION PURSUIT

Like the source of our feelings, the source of our passion is also frequently misinterpreted. Even by really smart people, such as the late Steve Jobs. There are many interviews of Jobs available on the Internet today. Most are quite informative and insightful. In one, though, Jobs says that finding and pursuing one's passion is the key to success. I disagree.

Jobs, of course, was a wildly successful person. But not because he found his dream job in Apple. It was because he was a wildly passionate person. The ability to be passionate rests within us; it doesn't depend on the perfect career, mate, lifestyle, outcome, or anything on the outside.

I got an unexpected peek at this perspective on passion this past July. I was on my way to a presentation and stopped at a Denny's restaurant in Vineland, New Jersey, for a quick breakfast. I sat at the counter, where I had a direct view into the kitchen.

Now, Vineland isn't the most glamorous town in which to live or work. It's seen its share of setbacks, most recently a tornado that ravaged numerous homes, businesses, and yards. That morning, however, Denny's was packed and the kitchen was cranking at breakneck speed. And as it did, the head chef set an awe-inspiring example of passion while also revealing the powerlessness of external circumstances.

He led his team of four chefs as if he were running a trading floor on Wall Street or a football team preparing for the Super Bowl. Amid the chaos of a bustling kitchen, this team was so engaged that their performance and food were flawless. Even in an extremely hot work environment (it was ninety-five outside and I could feel the heat of the kitchen from the counter), they churned out meal after meal with smiles on their faces and the occasional outburst of laughter.

But why? By all appearances, working in the kitchen of a Denny's restaurant in Vineland is about as dead-end as it gets. Why in the world would this cooking crew pour so much love, vigor, and determination into its work?

The answer, as you're now aware, lies in the fact that passion is created from in to out, never out to in. This crew's secret, I believe, was knowing that passion is an inside job— it's impervious to circumstance.

The same applies to you. If you lack passion, it's not because you're living, working, or studying in an undesirable environment; it's because you've created that environment in your own mind. By not understanding where your feelings originate, you're blaming circumstance, adding thought, and blocking the natural passion or energy that stimulates your system (more on the flow of energy, and passion, in chapter 3).

What are you supposed to do when this wayward perception occurs? Nothing. Knowing that it springs from your own thinking is as far as you need to look.

YOUR INNATE POTENTIAL AND MINE

Speaking of inside jobs, did you know that when you disagree with the actions of another person and get upset or frustrated, you possess the innate potential to quickly get over it, forgive, and then flourish?

It's true. Seeing that your upsets, frustrations, and judgments originate from within and only from within—just like your passion—is the first step down the path of no resistance, on the way to clarity and understanding.

An incident that occurred during my son Jackson's final high school baseball season, in the spring of 2012, provides a glimpse of this profound notion in action. Jackson, a team leader and one of the team's best players, got benched for supposed detrimental conduct. Nothing like that had ever happened to him before, and I threw myself on a train of judgmental thinking about Jackson's coach. For the next week, I went back and forth analyzing why the coach had made this decision. Was he out to show my son who was boss? Had my son become too big for his britches? How was this situation going to affect my son's college baseball future? As you can imagine, the more I worked myself into this frenzied mind-set, the worse I felt and the further from the truth I ventured.

For starters, my disquiet did not come from Jackson's coach or his decision. It came from attributing my bad feelings to Jackson's coach, when, in truth, they had come from inside of me. That said, we all get duped by our outside-in mirages, and for me at that moment, the situation was blurry.

This is why it's crucial to comprehend that your thinking is the sole source of your feelings. It's the difference between allowing yourself to become a casualty of uncontrollable circumstances and realizing that you're the one steering the ship. In other words, if you believe that your life situations are in charge—outside-in—you'll exist at the mercy of whatever happens to you. If you know that your thinking is in charge—inside-out—you'll naturally adapt from within (in spite of what happens to you) in order to retain your inner peace and perspective.

I did not, mind you, grow to like the coach's decision or agree with him. What I did was get my act together. I looked inward to the source of my feelings (my thinking) and ceased trying to make sense of the situation from such a revved-up state. My thinking then calmed, insights popped in, and I started to view things differently. Specifically, I recalled the many helpful things the coach had done for my son over the years.

There were other things that occurred to me as well. First: I might have been wrong. Second: Jackson was going to have an awesome season, no matter what. Last: Perhaps, like me, the coach wasn't seeing things clearly when he made this decision—a tendency that, from time to time, we all have in common.

Something else to keep in mind as we continue our dialogue about inside-out: Knowing that everyone creates their perceptions this way (from in to out) is always a great clarifier. As I stressed at the end of chapter 1, in spite of life history, intelligence, or personality, everyone's troubles are sourced from the same place: their thinking.

Here, then, are two quick inside-out suggestions that should provide instant clarity anytime you get stuck on a blurred train of judgment like I was:

- If you're upset, disagree with the actions of another person, and consider these actions to be the source of your feelings, it's you who isn't seeing things clearly.

- The potential always rests within you, no matter how disturbing a situation looks, to feel differently about it—without doing something about it.

WHY ATHLETES (AND NONATHLETES) CHEAT

Have you ever wondered why an athlete, or anyone for that matter, would cheat? Is it because of greed, a faulty value system, an overblown ego, past experiences, the pressure of the culture in which they work?

As you might be aware, the past two decades have seen a rash of performance-enhancing drug (PED) scandals in

Major League Baseball. But what's interesting is that the players implicated in these scandals possess varying character profiles. Some are brash; some reticent. Some come from affluence; some poverty. Some are generous with their time and money; some not so much. Plus, the same baseball culture exists for all players.

What is it then? Why do certain baseball players steer clear of cheating, and why do some try to beat the system?

It all comes back to the principle of thought. Players who understand that their feelings come from their thinking (from its ebb and flow), and not from their circumstances, will rarely cheat. These players make sound decisions because they recognize that there's no external reason why on occasion they might feel insecure, anxious, or egotistical. By contrast, players who incorrectly attribute their feelings to their circumstances—their next contract, a batting title, fame, a win or a loss—are prone to cheating because the confusion created by this outside-in misunderstanding revs up their thinking, making them incapable of making sound decisions.

The PED scandals in baseball show what can happen when anyone believes that his or her feelings come from a seemingly disturbing situation on the outside, and then makes the mistake of doing something about the situation before his or her head clears.

This explains why some players go through periods when cheating seems illogical to them—and why sometimes it seems like a rational thing to do. From clarity, honesty is easy for everyone. From a head filled with thought, people feel bound up—and, again, those who attribute this bound-up feeling to their life situations will act deceitfully.

Here's another relevant question: Why do you suppose that threats of discipline, such as suspensions, seem to work for some players and not for others? The answer is that threats do not cause players to abide by rules. Players abide by rules (reasonably set rules) when their heads are clear, but struggle to do so when their heads are cluttered—no matter how many games or how much money the league threatens to take away.[4]

Our feelings come from inside of us, and nowhere else. Understand this and, when you struggle, it's easy to carry on and allow your insecurities to wither away on their own. Believing that your feelings come from the outside is both perplexing and enticing—it's a fraudulent belief that spawns fraudulent behavior.

THE WELL OF HAPPINESS

Think back on what William James portended. He feared that focusing on behavior (like cheating) to bring out the best in people would not work. More than one hundred

---

4. We'll pick up the topic of rules (and why they don't lead to behaviors that are more desirable) again in chapter 4.

years ago, he spoke to the misleading concept of looking at the human experience from an outside-in standpoint.

But we're still doing it, big time, today.

As a parent, coach, teacher, business leader, or friend—are you really fostering the free will, the ability to make wise choices, and the happiness that rest within those you care about? Within yourself? It's not your fault if you're not. Outside-in is so prevalent that almost always it's accepted as a matter of course.

Gretchen Rubin is the author of the best-selling book *The Happiness Project*. Here were some of her top tips for becoming happier at the start of 2013, as told to the *Today* show's Matt Lauer:

- Make your bed in the morning.

- Take time for warm and tender greetings and farewells.

- Surround yourself with pleasing scents.

For those who listen to Rubin's advice on attaining happiness, I see the likelihood for problems down the road. Her tips sound nice, and surely she means well, but once you turn toward outside-in, it's not easy to turn back. That's the danger in building your life around these outside-in fixes. The longer you walk down the wrong path, the more difficult it is to find the right one.

Do you know that many people, such as baseball players

who cheat, are convinced that if they make a lot of money and become well known they will automatically be happy? Or, if not happy, at least they won't worry so much? Wasn't it actor Jim Carrey who said that he wanted everyone in the world to get rich and famous so they could see that these external aspirations have nothing to do with happiness and security?

Several researchers, in fact, have shown that Carrey isn't far off. In one fascinating study conducted jointly by Northwestern University and the University of Massachusetts, a group of people were asked about their level of happiness before and after winning a large amount of money in the lottery. Another group were asked about their level of happiness before and after being involved in an accident that left them paralyzed.[5] Believe it or not, the study revealed that if on a scale of 0 to 5, you were a 2 and won the lottery—a year later, you would still be a 2. If you were a 4 and became paralyzed—a year later, you would still be a 4. So much for outside-in.

Quick question: Is the inherently neutral nature of both the world outside and what happens to you in the world outside starting to sink in?

If yes, cool. If no, hang in there. Because the extent to which you appreciate that it's all inside-out will ultimately

5. Philip Brickman and Dan Coates (Northwestern University) and Ronnie Janoff-Bulman (University of Massachusetts), "Lottery Winners and Accident Victims: Is Happiness Relative?" *Journal of Personality and Social Psychology* 36, no. 8 (1978): 917–927.

determine your level of resilience—and happiness. Said a different way, it's not winning the lottery or becoming permanently disabled that seals your fate; it's whether or not you see that the variability of your thinking is what determines your outlook on everything.

Let me give you a less acute example of the resilience of inside-out. I've met with hundreds of athletes who at various points in their careers have failed miserably. Each of them will admit that, at times, failure really bothers them. But other times (without trying to feel better), it doesn't. "Sometimes, I can see where the failure is pointing me," they might say. Meaning that, depending on their thinking and state of mind in the moment, the loss either makes sense or it's devastating.

It works the same way for accident victims who persevere. Knowing that circumstances are, at their root, neutral (even though it usually doesn't appear that way) is what prevents accident victims from panicking, forcing, and failing at those moments when things look bleak. It also shortens the duration of the low moments and reduces their frequency.

To be clear, I'm not diminishing the severity of accidents, or any loss for that matter. I'm just like you; my thoughts about sickness or health, and failure and success, do affect my feelings. But, again, it's only my thoughts that do this— and when left alone, thoughts have no staying power.

People who understand that their thinking informs their senses—the thought-feeling connection—look within for answers, and thus overcome. People who don't understand this connection look outside, and are thus vulnerable. You're never obliged to trust, or act upon, the thoughts that show up in your head. As the aforementioned study on happiness reveals, those who know this thrive; those who don't, falter. Come what may.

BE STILL: TWELVE INTUITIVE SIGNS OF A LOW STATE OF MIND

There is a central theme of this chapter, and it runs throughout this book: If resilience, well-being, and achievement are important to you, then it's advantageous to learn (or relearn) that you live in the feeling of your thinking (inside-out), not in the feeling of what happens to you (outside-in). In order to feel something, you must think it first.

Often, as people start to notice the virtue in this message, they wonder about the personal warning signs of a low psychological outlook—the mental state from which we're prone to futility and frustration as well as inept or aberrant behavior. We'll talk more about warning signs (feelings) in chapter 3, but, at this stage, here's a list that I hope you will find helpful.

What follows are twelve intuitive signs that you might be making decisions, changes, or corrections from a depressed or unruly mind-set. And if so, it's time to ease off the gas and let things settle.

1. *You notice your thinking.*

   A productive state of mind, or clarity, is the result of fluent or undetectable thinking. Contentment, consistency, and success come from insight and instinct—not intellect.

2. *You feel bound up, anxious, or angry.*

   Feeling out of options, lacking confidence, and volatility are clear-cut signals that your inner vision is temporarily distorted. Insecurity is a normal result of the fact that you think—it's not related to the events of your life.

3. *You blame your circumstances for the way you feel.*

   Whether you grasp it by now or not, all people discern the world from the inside-out. The way you feel about your circumstances is determined by the fluctuations of your own thinking. That's why you'll perceive the exact same circumstance differently from moment to moment.

4. *You judge other people.*

   Judgment is the effect of a cluttered mind-set; it has nothing to do with other people or their actions. From a high state of mind, you'll have compassion and understanding for the same person you'll judge and disrespect from a low state of mind.

5. *You keep looking outside of yourself for answers.*

   If you're on a constant quest for fulfillment, jumping from relationship to relationship, team to team,
   school to school, city to city, guru to guru, self-help
   technique to . . . you get the idea, then you're only
   preventing your level of consciousness from ascend-
   ing on its own. If allowed to sit still, a glass of
   murky water always becomes clear.

6. *You try to think positively.*

   I can't say this enough: Those who understand
   the randomness of thought almost never try to
   change or fix their thinking. If you combat negative
   thoughts by trying to override them with positive
   ones, you only energize the negativity.

7. *You take things personally.*

   When your state of mind is low, you'll take things
   to heart and become sensitive and defensive. When
   your state of mind is high, just the opposite. It's
   okay to feel vulnerable, but don't forget: It's got
   nothing to do with the actions of others.

8. *You focus on illness and not health.*

   Waging a continuous battle to overcome your perceived deficits is like fighting a paper tiger. From a

clear mental outlook, you'll recognize your innate health and empower it. When frantic, you'll detect illness, and, if you buy in, it becomes the standard.

9. *You are intimidated or afraid.*

Fear is a sensation to which we instinctively respond to in the moment—with no thought or tension. If you're thinking about another person or situation and are intimidated, then what you're thinking is a self-created illusion born from a momentarily low psychological perspective.

10. *You believe you'll feel better when . . .*

Milestones have no ability to regulate your level of satisfaction or joy. Your state of mind creates your experience; your experience (fortune, fame, health) cannot alter your state of mind.

11. *You can't find your passion.*

As I explained earlier, you'll be passionate when your mood is elevated; passionless when it's deflated. So, when you lack drive or enthusiasm, don't look to your life for the why and wherefore. Young children are passionate and wondrous about everything. Why? Because clarity and consciousness are their norm.

12. *You practice awareness, mindfulness, or happiness.*
    Often, this final sign is misunderstood and looked
    at in reverse. If you practice awareness, mindfulness,
    or happiness, you turn built-in processes into forced
    strategies that require thought—and an excess of
    thought is what takes us out of awareness, mindful-
    ness, or happiness.

Understanding that there is a direct link between your
current mind-set and perceptions of everything is the real
key to enlightenment.

TRYING TO ACCEPT? IT'S OKAY IF YOU CAN'T

Let's take a close look at another built-in process: acceptance.
Acceptance—like awareness, mindfulness, and happiness—
does not need to be worked on. Over the past few years,
I've heard so many self-help experts, coaches, and spiritual
teachers promote "acceptance" as a deliberate practice that I
can't resist adding my two cents—from the inside-out.

In November 2012, for example, I watched author
Eckhart Tolle suggest to Oprah Winfrey on the Oprah
Winfrey Network that acceptance of a troubling situation is
the first rung toward effective action and change.

I don't see it working that way.

To me, the focus on acceptance is another hollow symptom of the outside-in disconnect. The more you try to

accept a so-called difficult life situation, the more attention you're placing on something that has nothing to do with the way you feel in the first place. By suggesting the strategy of acceptance, Tolle and others are looking outward to one's circumstances to explain one's feelings, when, as you know, the source of one's feelings is one's thinking.

You've also heard me say that it's impossible to make someone do something, or feel something, that the person doesn't think or feel. Meaning, you can't force someone into a certain disposition—not even yourself.

Here's an illustration using acceptance as our guinea pig: If you suffer the loss of a loved one and your thoughts are aggrieved, overwhelmed, or "unaccepting," looking to your loss and then trying to accept it will only fill your jam-packed head with more thoughts, thereby escalating your anguish. But if you don't take the outside-in approach, if you don't concentrate on accepting your tragedy, the loss will lose its gnawing grip.

Why? Because the true source of your feelings becomes obvious. Even in the midst of the loss, you don't always feel out of sorts, do you? That's because you're not feeling the loss. Your feelings come from inside of you—from your own thinking.

Recall the three main components of the inside-out paradigm, the central theme of this chapter:

- You live in the feeling of your thinking.

- Your perceptions are formed from the inside-out.

- There isn't a cause-and-effect relationship between your circumstances and feelings.

That's why trying to do something about your circumstances for the purpose of feeling better simply doesn't work. Have you ever gone through a low period in your life and tried to change or accept your career, house, hairstyle, or mate because you identified this external circumstance as the basis for your low feelings? I bet that didn't work out as planned, did it?

It can't work any other way. Any time a self-help method requires doing, fixing, or accepting (actually, I've never seen a self-help method that doesn't), it does so in complete disregard for the state of mind of the person in question. People are just not capable of accepting anything when their thinking is bound up and, as a result, they are suffering. People are always capable, though, of understanding why they feel bad—their thinking, not their life, has hit a hurdle and trended lower.

And, by the way, you're never obligated to do anything with your bad feelings. You simply need to remember that, by design, the impact of all thoughts (feelings and then moods) has a minimum shelf life.

YOUR ILLUSIONARY PAST

Our perceptions are thought dependent. Free-and-easy thinking turns life wondrous and appealing; bound-up thinking turns life restrictive and ominous. Most of us, however, make the mistake of neglecting the implications of this principle when it comes to the past.

It's not your fault. At times, even my wife, Liz (who has a clear understanding of the inside-out paradigm), innocently connects past experiences with present feelings. One night, when I came home in a bad mood, a worried Liz inquired, "What's the matter?"

I replied, "Nothing, babe."

She then insisted, "C'mon, what happened in the office today? There has to be something."

But was there? When you struggle, should you look to your past (immediate or otherwise) to formulate the reason or the excuse? Should you look to your past to find the cure? The answer, as you probably figured, is no. Your *memories* of the past are just *thinking* that's accumulated over a period of time. Your past is not real now; your past exists outside of you. And your feelings aren't created from anything outside of you. It works inside-out across the board.

The self-help world disagrees with me on this one, too. Virtually all therapists and counselors believe, and have been trained to believe, that conquering former distress is the key to overcoming current distress. They often insist that the clue to finding truth is going back to the past, to those haunting times, and resolving or forgiving former traumas. This, alas, is the type of backward thinking that *revs up* people's heads, fueling their restlessness.

Let's try simplicity. When people delve into their pasts to rationalize current struggles, they seek answers in the same sea of misinformation that created the troubles in the first place. As Sydney Banks once said, "Going back to a troubled past is like putting your hand in a fire, pulling it out because it burns, and then putting it back in so it can heal."

My own experience with depression—as described in the introduction—is a good example of this. During that period, I scrutinized my past looking for answers. But this became confounding, since at times I loathed my childhood, yet at other times it seemed just fine. In fact, the more I tried to connect present-day feelings to past events, the worse things got. Then, out of the blue, it struck me: If I thought about my past one day and felt bad, and I thought about my past another day and felt good, my past must not have anything to do with the way I felt. There had to be something inside of me that was causing my despair or happiness.

Right then and there, it no longer made sense that my childhood had the ability to hurt me. There could only be one thing that was producing my feelings: the variable makeup of my own thinking.

Incidentally, I do understand the desire to fix. Like Liz (who was concerned about my low mood), you want the best for your family, friends, and yourself. Liz prodded, lovingly, only because she cares. But, remember, my state of mind had nothing to do with circumstance. I walked into the house that night randomly stuck in thought and, consequently, not feeling myself. At that moment, the worst thing to do was search outside. If I tried hard enough, I could have found at least twenty things about my day in the office, or life in general, to brood over.

Instead, we simply sat down to dinner. And by the time we were done, the troubles of the day had vanished.

TIME AND YOUR STATE OF MIND

If our memories are nothing more than perpetual thoughts carried from one moment to the next, maybe it's a good idea to talk about the impression of time as a whole. After all, many scientists have tried to explain time, and there are many theories about it.

Have you ever wondered about time? I have. When I find myself daydreaming, feeling good, and lost in imagination (whether while playing sports, writing, or relaxing with my family), something eerie sometimes occurs: It feels like the past, present, and future are all happening at once. I know, it sounds kind of "out there." But what if this eerie phenomenon could help us not only better understand time, but human nature as well?

Think about it (not too hard, please): When your head

is cluttered and you're unable to lose yourself in imagination, doesn't time seem to fragment, as you feel trapped in the past, resistant to the present, and concerned about the future? For many people, time is a burden. Perhaps we've been approaching time from the wrong direction: outside-in rather than inside-out.

To illustrate, I once had a string of conversations with a football player who, in his words, was coming off the worst season of his career. Due to injuries and personal issues, he believed that his entire life had been set back a year.

But I told him that just wasn't so: "I'm certain that the events of this year are setting the stage for your future development as a player and a person. These situations—your feelings, too—aren't meant to get in your way; they're meant to show you the way." I maintained that his current thinking was obscuring his perception of time. I pointed him inward.

At first, he looked at me curiously. But, as he turned away from circumstance, I sensed tranquility and relief flooding in. His perception of the past and future then started to clear.

He spoke about how, since he couldn't practice or travel with the team, he had rededicated himself to his wife and family. He mentioned that watching home games from the team skybox as he recuperated gave him a different perspective on his teammates, opponents, and the game in general. He went on to say, "It's crazy, but now my injury and all that happened to me last year kind of make sense. I can envision how my growth as a person off the field is already contributing to my success on the field next season."

At that moment, by all appearances, the past, present, and future were playing out simultaneously in this player's mind. The events of the previous season hadn't changed. But his thinking had, and so had his level of clarity—and faith.

This far-out idea of time is worth considering. As our thoughts turn lucid, we make sense of the past, engage the present, and visualize the future with ease. So, I ask you: Is it possible that the past, present, and future have all happened already and they're not in our control? Are we really *that* free?

Many of the top athletes with whom I work often hint at this type of experience, sometimes calling it "the zone." And while they have trouble describing this feeling, they talk about getting swept away in the stillness or nothingness from which inspired performance comes easy. To me, though, it's simple: Human beings are at their best when the intellect shuts off and insights and energy have room to flow. That's why you occasionally experience déjà vu or find yourself in the right place at the right time without effort.

So far in *The Path of No Resistance*, I've alluded to the fact that all sensory experience, including the natural high of the zone, comes from thought—or a lack thereof. I've also said that thought is a spiritual principle. Yet if you remain sketchy about where our football player's clarity came from, and why he envisioned future success, try this on for size: His brain went silent, so he momentarily escaped the boundaries of time and the world of form in which he lives.

Inside-out is all-encompassing. Any answer past that is way beyond my pay grade.

TWELVE REAL REASONS WHY YOU FEEL LOW AND SHOULD STOP LOOKING OUTSIDE

Amazing and sometimes uncanny possibilities begin to open up once we recognize the powerless complexion of circumstance. Readily, the perpetual field expands, and we find ourselves a few steps ahead of the competition. The reason that President Obama is such a good debater is the same reason that tennis great Roger Federer often tracks down balls out of nowhere, and the same reason that chef Bobby Flay seems to sniff out optimum restaurant locations that others miss: To them, external influences don't amount to much. These three live life from the inside-out. They are consistent. They are conscious. They are resilient.

The same gift rests within you. Yes, intellect and life experiences do combine to meld personality. But there's *nothing personal* about the thought-feeling connection. It works alike for everyone. A circumstance can't make us feel a certain way because a circumstance-feeling connection does not exist.

If you're game, answer these two questions for me: When you watch an intense or emotional movie, do you fight the experience? Or does your thinking get silent and you embrace the ride? Well, your life is no different. If at this point you see, even a little bit, that all experience is created from the inside-out—I promise, you're on your way.

To sum up chapter 2, the following list provides twelve examples of why, at times, you (President Obama, Federer, and Flay, too) have trouble shaking an unhappy, vague, or insecure mind-set. What to do about these mind-sets—as you'll see coming up—that's the easy part.

1. You forget that errant thoughts are normal, thus you try to change your thoughts.

2. You accept your errant thoughts as real, thus you try to change your thoughts.

3. You focus on what you're thinking about, not the fact that you think.

4. You try to fix troublesome life situations from a temporarily low psychological perspective.

5. You jump from one external fix or coping mechanism to another.

6. You use your intellect to search for answers, when answers are found via insight (from within).

7. You fight your experiences, when you should be having experiences.

8. You attribute your feelings to your circumstances, when they're purely the result of your thinking.

9. You use your feelings as a life-indicator, when they're only a thinking-indicator (more on this in chapter 3).

10. You overlook the fact that problems aren't the cause of your lows; they're a symptom of them.

11. You are convinced that experience creates state of mind, when state of mind creates experience.

12. You believe that willpower (battling through your lows) is the appropriate and commendable response, when knowing that the human mind is designed to return to clarity on its own is the only response that fosters your innate functioning and consciousness.

———

There is another thing I want to repeat prior to chapter 3: Believing that your circumstances have the power to make you feel a certain way (outside-in) is normal, so don't panic when this occurs. It's merely the byproduct of living in a world of form. Nevertheless, knowing that your feelings come from your thinking (inside-out) is what allows you to navigate proficiently through this world of form.

Here's a final example, also from the sports world, of inside-out versus outside-in—and how understanding that your experience is shaped from in to out makes life a whole lot simpler.

At the end of the 2012 NFL season, I heard current football analyst and former New York Giants quarterback Phil Simms talk on WFAN radio in New York about the changing weather patterns in the New York area. Simms said that back when he played (1980 to 1993), the winds were so bad in Giants Stadium that he made the deliberate decision to lower his personal expectations since it was so difficult to throw the ball.

Yet to Simms's surprise, when he interviewed current Giants quarterback and two-time Super Bowl MVP Eli Manning, and asked him about the difficult winds in New York, Manning didn't know what Simms was talking about. According to Manning, "I've never played a home game when the wind was a problem, not ever."

Simms is a good analyst, and, if my memory serves me correctly, he was a durable player. But in this case, he's looking outside to the weather—a circumstance—to explain his feelings, experience, and perceptions. Manning knows, intuitively, that doing so is a mistake.

As we continue to peel away the half-truths about what determines resilience, remember: At this very moment, every single person alive, including you, is searching for a secure feeling. But, like Simms, when you don't feel secure, you're also prone to making the innocent but caustic error of looking outside to explain the reason. Excuses then over-work your intellect, making you feel and perform worse.

Rather, the missing link between your circumstances and a secure feeling is always found in your thinking. Not in what you think. Just knowing that your reality is formed from the inside-out, via your thinking, is what allows the mind's immune system (your psychological immune system) to bring you back to assurance and faith.

In my many years of working with people, and writing and speaking about why human beings feel what we feel and do what we do, my conclusion is that outside-in is a confounding entity. Explanations and solutions cannot be found in form. So when you look outside, you manufacture, validate, and perpetuate problems that don't really exist. If you keep looking that way (in your desire to make sense of things and feel better), there's no end to the distorted perceptions or potential mayhem that could occur.

Sadly, most of us have it backwards. Outside-in is not how it works. Since long before William James, there's been a misalignment between how people think they experience life, and what's really happening behind the scenes in their heads. My aim in this book is to straighten out that misalignment.

We've made some progress, but let's keep going.

3.

YOUR INTUITIVE GUIDE

"When I find myself in times of trouble, Mother Mary comes to me, speaking words of wisdom, let it be. And when the night is cloudy there is still a light that shines on me, shine on until tomorrow, let it be."

—*"Let It Be," The Beatles*

I once heard Syd Banks say that wisdom is everywhere: "It's in our libraries, our religions, the arts, on billboards, even in the grocery store." Syd claimed that we are hiding from wisdom; wisdom is not hiding from us. The trick, though, is to know what to look for.

I must have listened to the Beatles' "Let It Be" five hundred times before I finally realized where John Lennon and Paul McCartney were guiding us: to the self-corrective power of the human mind. Before that, my outside-in misunderstanding didn't permit me to see truth, even when it stared right back at me.

Today, I remind myself of the significance of "letting it

be" when I get indignant in my own thinking. Everyone is doing the best they can to the degree that they see the role of thought in their life. We each have a different perspective on the source of our feelings, and that perspective can switch on a dime.

Think back, again, to the "acuity gap" (see chapter 1). This is the distance between our perception of a circumstance and the moment we see that the circumstance has no power—that it's neutral—since our feelings can only come from thought. As I expressed, it works the same for all of us. No one is more grounded in this principle than anyone else. The extent of our errant thinking at any particular moment always accounts for our outlook.

This is why, for no apparent reason, "mean" people or bullies sometimes turn compassionate. They get distracted from their depressed thinking, their thinking clears out, and, by design, compassion fills the space—until their thinking (not their life) churns up again. Even those whom the mental health establishment classifies as "psychotic" occasionally show glimpses of lucidity or love. The potential for mental health, therefore, rests within every person. We've just been focusing our efforts in an outside-in direction—on behavior, the past, or a genetic diagnosis instead.

Much can be accomplished when we look at mental health through the lens of inside-out. Here's an illustration. Perhaps the most touching moment of my career occurred when I received a call a short time after I wrote *Stillpower*.

The call was from a seventh-grade teacher in New Mexico named Maria Venegas. Maria, who is also an athlete, originally bought *Stillpower* to improve her sports performance. But after reading the book, she became most interested in the chapter where I discussed bullying. Bullying, I'm sorry to say, was running rampant in her classroom and school.

Maria wanted to learn more about my inside-out approach, primarily with regard to feelings. She asked if I believed that "feelings" held the key to healing the bullying epidemic. I told her she was on the right path.

I explained to Maria that current anti-bullying protocols, while well intended, make matters worse. Telling students in the midst of dysfunctional thinking—the only reason a person would bully or fall prey to one—to be respectful and considerate, or brave and resolute, is nothing but a recipe for more dysfunctional thinking and thus disaster. As we've seen, overthinking is what distorts perceptions and behavior. Codes of conduct require students to think more.

Rather, we must teach students (adults, too) that feelings actually have a divine purpose: They're our intuitive guide, our navigational instrument. We feel our thinking. So it's our feelings that let us know if our thinking is helpful or hurtful, or if we're seeing life with understanding or disdain. For example, if I disagree with the actions of one of my friends, my feelings are telling me if I've got a bona fide gripe or not. If I feel insecure and angry, I don't. If I feel secure and composed, I do. Inside-out never fails.

Back to Maria. I said to her, "If you can show your students that as their feelings move up and down, so will their judgments of each other, bullying just might cease."

What happened next is beyond description in words, but I'll do my best. Maria had an insight: She developed a device called a "mood chart," which she hung on the wall in her classroom. The "moods" ranged from love to hate, from happiness to misery, from compassion to judgment. Each morning, her students put a magnet next to the mood on the chart that best described their feelings. They did this five times throughout the day.

Now, Maria didn't tell her class why she created the mood chart. That's the best part of her insight. She *allowed* the students' free will and instincts to burgeon, and slowly but surely—as the students started to see that with each trip to the mood chart their feelings changed for no outside reason—she noticed marked behavioral improvement. Pretty soon, bullying in Maria's classroom stopped and was replaced with kindness, cooperation, and spirit. The rest of the school then adopted the mood chart, with similar successful results. When Maria phoned to tell me what happened, I was reduced to tears.

———————

This story reveals the innate power of looking inward for answers. Bullies bully when they attribute their insecure feelings to something other than the natural ebb and flow of their thinking. When a bully looks outside to cope with these feelings, the nearest person often gets caught in the crossfire.

By contrast, when Maria's students noticed that their feelings changed independent of the actions of others, intuitively, they had two realizations:

- The students found that no matter what they thought and felt about a classmate in the moment, there was always an opportunity to see the same classmate differently.

- Believing that "I have to fix you in order to fix me" no longer seemed logical. Bullying someone who had nothing to do with the way a student felt in the first place would not help anyone.

What's more, one of Maria's students even declared, "Learning that our feelings on the inside are the cause of our views of people on the outside, and not the other way around, changed everything for our class and school." But, more important, she went on, "If everyone could learn this, the world would be transformed forever."

Maria Venegas, my friends, is a superstar.

WORRY, INSIGHT, AND WHY YOU NEED TO KNOW THE DIFFERENCE

The genius of the mood chart is that Maria had an extraordinary insight as to the effect it would have on her classroom. However, I don't recommend it, indiscriminately, as a model. The mood chart worked for Maria because she understands inside-out. Remember: This book isn't about subscribing to models; it's about intuitively building your own.

Yes, bullying in her school was serious business, current methods weren't working, and something needed to be done. But when it comes to bullying, it's easy to get anxious or desperate because it looks so much like we're feeling the gravity of the circumstance. Maria knew that just wasn't so.

Many people, in fact, think that the supposed significance, or seriousness, of certain situations has something to do with how they feel. A business executive might say, "I get that I create my own perceptions of a rainy day, but this business deal is important. I'm worried about it because if I mess it up, I'm screwed." The athletes with whom I work do it, too. Most can easily get over a regular season loss, but a loss in the playoffs, now that's a catastrophe.

But it doesn't add up. You can't pick and choose which life events are perceived from the inside and which are perceived from the outside. As we've learned so far, you feel the randomness of your thinking, not the randomness of how things turn out. And knowing this is what makes a person resilient. Knowing this turns a person inward to the source of clarity, calm, and insight.

Not seeing it? Are you convinced that we live in a mixed paradigm, or that both a thought-feeling connection and a circumstance-feeling connection exist? Do you believe, for example, that worrying about "meaningful" circumstances represents a conscientious state of mind? Almost all people do. Take most parents. They consider fretting about their kids a sign of responsibility. Well, fretting about one's kids isn't right or wrong, but it has nothing to do with being responsible—or making practical choices for kids, for that matter.

Let's set the record straight by defining the difference between worry and insight. Once again, the thought-feeling connection is the key.

> Worry: *The process of feeling persistently uneasy about things.*

> Insight: *The process of grasping the hidden nature of things.*

For sure, it's common to mistake your worries for insights. Everyone does it. You have an innocent thought about a circumstance, the thought produces an uneasy feeling, and you deduce (because of the uneasy feeling) that your thought has merit and needs consideration. Yet the opposite is true: An uneasy feeling—a worry—is a sign that what you're thinking in the moment has no merit and should not be considered.

All people, moreover, possess the capacity for both worry and insight. People worry when, from a temporarily low outlook, they make assumptions about the future. Insights, on the other hand, do predict the future. They're void of revved-up thinking; they feel free and uncomplicated. As Maria Venegas's mood chart showed, insights lead to productive decisions and actions.

Why is it so important to know the difference between worries and insights? Hmm, have you ever noticed how worries grow when we feed them with attention and belief? For example, let's say I schedule a lunch date with Liz and she's late. I harmlessly think, "I hope she didn't get into an accident." The thought then makes me feel anxious, so I hoodwink myself into believing that the situation—a conjured-up accident—is serious enough to be the reason for my feelings.

The tension swells: "I told her she needed to leave on time; she was probably rushing; when she rushes, she loses concentration; when people lose concentration, they get in accidents; oh my God, I hope the accident isn't serious."

Sound familiar? Here's what you need to know to avoid one of these thought-constructed chain reactions: My pre-worrisome thought, "I hope she didn't get into an accident," was not what caused my distress. Confusing it for an insight is what did this. In the moment, I simply failed to heed the thought-feeling connection. The feeling of insecurity was my intuitive sign that my initial thought about the future was unreliable. It was a false impression, an assumption, a worry—not an insight. And it works the same for you.

The difference between worry and insight, then, can be summed up like this:

worry and its feeling of uneasiness = illusion

insight and its feeling of calm = truth

Meanwhile, if you're thinking that there was a chance that Liz could have been in an accident, I agree. But that's called coincidence. When insights happen, there's no chance or luck involved. Life carries out as contemplated, and, instinctively, we know just what to do.

A MAGIC BULLET?

It's both fundamental and critical to recognize that your feelings are guiding you. We're often told, in error, that the content of our thoughts serve this purpose: "Be aware of your thoughts." "Thoughts become things." "Thoughts are a window to one's soul." These sayings are just a few examples of this misunderstanding.

The truth is that everyone thinks some pretty crazy

thoughts now and again. I know that some of the things that pop into my head are just ridiculous. Thoughts also happen too fast to catch—particularly, as my lunch-date example showed, when we try to manage or control them. Feelings, however, are impossible to ignore and easy to pin down. *Feel* the slightest bit of resistance and, rest assured, you're on the wrong path.

Consider the simple act of dropping a candy wrapper on the ground. In spite of being informed about the negative environmental effects of littering, many people still do it. But, be honest, how do you feel when you litter? You sense that there's something off about it, don't you? Your feelings are your guide.

Or how about one of the situations I mentioned in the introduction of this book? If you get cut off on a highway and feel angry and vulnerable, are your unstable feelings telling you to confront the other driver, or to drive on? *Keep driving.* If it were appropriate to confront the other driver, your gut wouldn't feel twisted and you wouldn't hesitate—you'd simply do it. Isn't it amazing how obvious answers become once you understand the intention of feelings?

Several of my clients, in fact, have told me that relief set in for them after they learned about feelings. Mistakenly, they have been trying to fight through their feelings for years. Yet often these clients wonder why—since the mind is designed to self-correct—they don't immediately feel better when they turn away from a circumstance such as being cut off on a highway. They might ask, "If I forget that a circumstance doesn't account for my feelings and try to do something about it in order to feel better, it makes sense that I would end up feeling worse. But if I don't do this, if I look inward, why does it sometimes take so long for my feelings to improve?"

The answer is: Understanding the principle of thought, and its relationship to your feelings, isn't like drinking a cup of coffee to kick-start your day. It won't necessarily jolt your feelings back to serenity. But, as I made plain in chapter 1, it will prevent you from turning your life upside down. So, using the highway example again, if you choose to continue driving—and not cope with your feelings—you might seethe for the next mile or two, but by the time you get to your destination, the incident will be forgotten.

Allowing clarity to rise to the surface on its own is paramount. There's no magic bullet to reach for when those anxious moments appear. Even using common strategies such as "try to understand what the other person is going through" or "remain calm and count to ten" won't provide long-term relief. Why? Because such fixes place more thought into your already revved-up mind.

Michael Neill, my colleague and the author of *The Inside-Out Revolution*, summarizes the myth of mind strategies by using the analogy of getting thrown into a lake and clinging to a log as opposed to floating. Keep clinging and both you and the log will sink.

The way I see it, fixing a thought-created perception by applying an externally created cure is like putting a trap under your bed to catch a monster. It only legitimizes and bolsters your fearful thoughts. Yet, like a young child who wails one minute and smiles the next, the more you rely on your mind's intuitive ability to self-correct—the more you empower it. Looking toward the thought-feeling connection, and away from the illusionary presence of a circumstance-feeling connection, is what opens the door to resilience, ease, and efficiency.

You know what? Maybe we *are* born with a magic bullet after all. It's called our feelings.

AVOIDING CRISIS

Indeed, feelings are our magic bullet. I remember the poignant moment when this wisdom became crystal clear to my son Ryan, and it deepened my understanding as well.

It was a normal Sunday morning at home. I was in the basement, working out in our home gym, when I overheard Liz and Ryan, who was thirteen at the time, arguing upstairs. Things were getting pretty heated, so I decided to play peacemaker. I walked up the stairs, opened the door a crack, and said, "What's going on up here?" Ryan, who unbeknownst to me was standing nearby, then angrily slammed the door shut, hurling me downward. He heard me fall and opened the door just in time to see me grab on to the handrail at the bottom and right myself. I wasn't injured, but I was shocked, and furious at Ryan. Inside-out is *not* how this experience felt at that moment.

What I've found in tumultuous moments like this is that most parents would say something along these lines: "You need to be respectful; you have no right to talk to your mother like that."

And as their thinking revved up even more: "How could you slam the door in your father's face? You need to learn a lesson—you're grounded!"

Now, by no means am I a perfect father. Occasionally, I play victim to my thinking like everyone else, but not this time. I knew that Ryan's level of respect for his parents, right then, was the result of whether or not he noticed that he was feeling his thinking, not the circumstance. Respect can't be instilled from the outside. This was a growth opportunity for Ryan, and me, not an opportunity to dictate.

We calmly sat together and went through the purpose of feelings. We talked about what happens when a person looks to anything external to account for them.

"I can't believe I did that," Ryan said. That's when I reminded him that a bound-up mind-set is not what causes crisis; acting from one is the culprit. I even proved this principle by revealing to Ryan how it had just played out for me: If getting pushed down the stairs had been the true source of my fury, I would have still felt that way and, more than likely, would have focused on Ryan's behavior in an attempt

THE PATH OF NO RESISTANCE

to fix my feelings. If I had acted from a bound-up mind-set and chosen that outward direction, I wouldn't have quelled the crisis; I would have provoked it. Ryan listened—and the love behind my words sank in.

The value in knowing that a well of fresh ideas and perspectives rests within you, and me, relates to everything. No matter the situation, when you understand the instinctive purpose of feelings, sullied thinking departs, solutions arise without effort, and crises become opportunities.

What did I want Ryan to realize that day? That his feelings don't lie. They're his intuitive defense mechanism, steering him away from any and all misguided thoughts—always.

TAKE A RISK, OR BOLDLY MOVE FORWARD?

Everyone gets indecisive, but not due to circumstance. Indecision is a normal byproduct of a surplus of personal thought, an intellect on overload. It's the ultimate sign that your thinking is not your friend in the moment. But, as it did for my son, your newfound understanding about your feelings (if you listen to them) will pave the way to clear thinking and certainty.

Astute choices result from the free-and-easy feeling of your own insights. Unfortunately, misinformation is constant. Outside forces (your parents, teachers, coaches, or employer) are judging, urging, and pushing in order to bring out your best. Your best isn't cultivated like that, however.

For lasting success, a person's instincts and inner wisdom must be the only source of inspiration.

While doing research for this book, I wandered onto a website where a popular self-help author posted this outside-in message: "Making progress involves risk. Period. You can't make it to second base with your foot on first."

We've heard it all before: Don't sit on your hands. Don't let the grass grow under your feet. Or, from one of my favorite movies, *Hoosiers*, "Don't get caught watching the paint dry." But these directives, like the one from our self-help author, overlook something noteworthy: Sometimes we're just better off staying put. When you take a risk, you run the risk of stifling insight and thus bringing out the worst—not the best—in yourself and others.

Contrary to popular opinion, then, you're not a coward if you see a chance and don't take it. Actually, the inner sensation of risk has a profound purpose: It tells you that you're not seeing things clearly at that moment, so don't act! For a baseball player who's on first base and is tempted to steal second, a hesitant feeling means that he's supposed to hold the bag.

Making progress has nothing to do with risk. We advance when we act from an instinctual sense of conviction; we regress when we sense apprehension and decide to act anyway. That's that.

As an illustration, golf legend Arnold Palmer was a player who always went for broke. The word "charge" was often associated with Palmer, since if there was a chance to take, he was up for the dare. But this propensity to not listen to his uncertain feelings—the feelings of risk—cost Palmer far more tournaments than he won.

By contrast, one of Palmer's main rivals, Jack Nicklaus, also appeared to take chances at times on the golf course. Nicklaus, however, understood that his feelings emerged from the inside-out. He once said, "The biggest rival I had in my career was me."[6] His astounding success is proof that the apparent chances he took weren't chances at all. They were insights instead.

This is not to say that successful people, such as Nicklaus, don't experience precarious feelings from time to time—we all do. My message is that when we act from precarious feelings, as Palmer sometimes did on the golf course, we potentially find trouble. A key difference between steadiness and inconsistency is that steady people become still and then find another option when they sense danger. Inconsistent people try to exhibit strength by plowing through it.

No matter the circumstance, it's never a specific behavior, like taking risks, that determines your level of success or failure. It's the feeling state from which you behave.

In spite of what others might say, then, the next time you're tempted to steal second base, consider: You'll get there easily if you run boldly but free; you'll get tagged out if you feel the slightest sense of risk.

MAKING CHANGE HAPPEN

A quick reminder: It's not necessary for you to practice awareness or stand on guard for your feeling state moment to moment. In chapter 2, I said that you don't want to turn an intuitive process into a rote and rigid exercise. Jack Nicklaus didn't consciously ask himself how he was feeling before every shot, or if he was aware. No. He understood that even in the heat of competition, he lived in the feeling of his thinking. So he rarely overanalyzed or got in the way of his instincts. That's why he won—a lot.

For long-term peace of mind, looking inward toward the thought-feeling connection is the first and only step. I often tell my audiences to look there, and let life take care of itself. However, if you're still convinced that in order to find clarity, wisdom, and answers, you must practice awareness or do something else externally—like seek out a guru, climb a far-off mountain, or try meditation—then listen up.

There's a pivotal difference between doing something— the act of meditation, for example—and finding a naturally meditative state. When a person's intellect quiets, answers automatically rise to the surface. But this wisdom unfolds from the inside. It doesn't enter because of something a person does on the outside. Ever.

That's why "Make change happen," a mantra used from boardrooms to locker rooms everywhere, is ineffective. Affirmative change is not the result of something we *make* happen from the outside. It's the result of a revelation from the inside, which is why we don't detect true transformations until *after* they've already occurred.

This wasn't a major transformation, but here's a demonstration of the rearview-mirror nature of change: I was once having a rough morning at work when, without warning, I found myself sitting in a comfortable chair in the lobby of our office building. I didn't scrutinize the decision to do this. I don't even remember planning to walk there. I had acted without thinking. A respite was needed, so instinctively, not tactically, I just took it. And it totally worked. My angst left me, and the rest of my day turned out great.

Go back to the weight-loss example. We know that the majority of people who attempt a diet plan fail to keep the weight off permanently. No matter the weight-loss strategy, the success rate is crazy low. Yet every now and then, a dieter finds permanent success. Why? Because in spite of the strategy's outside-in slant, the person's thinking becomes still enough (if only for a moment) for an insight to slip through. And insights, as you've read, wake people up by providing prompt changes of heart. They spur the kind of effortless action from which the person looks back and wonders, "How did I just pull *that* off?"

Feelings are how. Your feelings—and nothing on the outside—are always at work. They're holding your hand, guiding you away from insecure thinking (and stumbling blocks) and toward instinct and vision.

Are you starting to relate to the inborn purpose of feelings? Reflect for a second on the most enduring achievements of your own life. Did you force them? Did you strain? Or did you feel free as invention fell into your lap? Always, change for the better happens fluently, sans willpower.

With that in mind, here are two final examples of how feelings are meant to guide you away from making changes based on dysfunctional or desperate thinking. These examples should help us along our no-resistance path:

- In our home gym, we have a piece of equipment called a rowing machine. If you've ever used a rowing machine, you know that there are times when rowing feels like a struggle. But when this happens, your feelings aren't telling you to yank harder or quit. If either was the case, the impulse would be straightforward and your actions immediate. Your feelings are telling you to *ease* into the functioning of the machine. If you listen, the workout becomes a breeze.

- Early this year, I got a call from Rick, a former hockey player of mine from my high school coaching days. Rick was feeling down, and out of options. He and his family had moved from New Jersey to New Hampshire, and he was missing his friends back home. Having recently graduated from college, he was also working hard to find a job, but coming up empty. For the time being, Rick was packing groceries at a local market.

I told Rick that his down feelings were not a barometer of his life or future; they were a barometer of his thinking. We spoke for a while, and at the end of the call I reminded him, "The off feeling in your gut is simply a sign that you're not seeing things clearly. Distrust all thoughts and perceptions when you feel this way."

Rick called back the following week to thank me for pointing him toward his thinking and away from his circumstances (moving, job search). He now felt fine. But there were also two other things that he couldn't wait to mention: First, he had three job interviews in Boston coming up next month. Second, he had just started dating a cute girl who worked with him at the grocery store.

I asked if she was new at the grocery store. Rick's response: "Nope, she's been there longer than me. I just noticed her last week!"

Inside-out works like a charm. The cute girl was always there; Rick just wasn't able to see her. At all times, our feelings indicate how we are thinking—bound up or free—and what we should or shouldn't do next. When we listen to our feelings, our heads clear and the perceptual field (our awareness) expands without effort.

So let's keep looking in the liberating direction of feelings. From it, you're guaranteed to make the right kind of changes for yourself and the world around you. Why? With an absence of thought, you'll be acting from your own inner wisdom.

HARD WORK HAS NOTHING TO DO WITH IT

We all live in the steady up-and-down flow of our feelings. While everyone understands this to a certain degree, we each have specific circumstances in our lives—a past failure, an upcoming deadline, the behavior of family—that we habitually blame our feelings on. When we try to fix our feelings by addressing these circumstances, we falter since our feelings don't come from them. Have you ever, like Rick, worked hard to fix something because you thought it was the right thing to do, only to keep making bad judgments and falling short? I know I have, and the same goes for some of my former teammates and coaches.

My hockey coach at Hamilton College, Greg Batt, was a legend by the time I got there. He was one of the best

American-born players ever, and Hamilton's most tenured coach. Yet, while Coach Batt was great to play for when things were good, if we lost a few in a row—he could turn into a crazy person. I remember at one point during my sophomore year, we were on a bad losing streak, so Coach kept driving my teammates and me, working us harder and harder. We obliged, out of respect and fear (mostly fear), pushing ourselves to exhaustion and trying to fight our way to a win. But you know what? This particular slump became as legendary as Coach Batt—ten games of mistakes and barren efforts. It wasn't until Coach had pretty much thrown his hands up, and taken his foot off the gas pedal, that we turned things around.

Why did the hard-work prescription, in effect, make matters worse? Why didn't the idea of grinding it out lead to success? And why is this instinct-inhibiting direction so often promoted when, if you look closely, it just doesn't pay dividends? (As an aside, if you've experienced some success in your life and you think breaking your back is the cause, please reread the section in chapter 2 on passion.)[7]

The answers to these questions have to do with what truly initiates a slump. A slump occurs when a person looks outside for the source of his or her low feelings and tries to fight

---

7. More on hard work, and why it doesn't cause success, in the "Woods, Colvin, and Gladwell" section in chapter 4.

through these feelings, which results in a more bound-up psychological perspective. Trying to work even harder from this perspective only compounds the slump since you can't find a solution through the same hazy lens that created the problem to start with.

In the sales world, for example, the standard advice for an underperforming salesperson is to go out and sell harder or pound the pavement, so to speak. But since effort and fervor are a byproduct of a person's mind-set, the salesperson can pound away until hell freezes over and not cut it. From a low mind-set, his or her ability to perform and learn from mistakes remains limited. Not only that, the company's image may take a hit, since it has a lackluster salesperson representing it in public.

You know the old company line "The harder you work, the luckier you get," right? Well, it's not up to snuff. How hard you work is beside the point. The mind-set from which you work—now that's a different story. I've stood outside many a batting cage and watched baseball players work their tails off. Too often, though, a player will take swing after swing only to see his in-game productivity decline. Why? Slaving away at a performance problem holds *in place* the cluttered mind-set that established it. To the contrary, I've watched some of the most successful baseball players step into a batting cage prepared for a long workout, and only take a few swings. Now why do you think that is?

Here, then, is another pertinent formula to remember:

**any performer + a low state of mind =
the illusion of a performance problem**

How do you overcome a performance problem? Listen to your intuitive guide. There's nothing wrong with being diligent, determined, or even gung-ho. (I love giving it everything I've got, and I hope you do as well.) But *never* when your feelings are telling you otherwise.

Keep this in your sights from earlier: Ask top competitors to describe their feelings after triumphant performances, and they use simple words like *effortless, free,* and *automatic.* But how about this new wrinkle? Ask the same question of those who fall short, or finish second, and they say with exasperation, "I grinded as hard as I could. I worked my tail off. I tried my best, and that's all I can do."

But that's not so. It's always exhausting to fight through your instincts. What you can do is understand where effort and excellence truly stem from: the freedom and inspiration available when you look within to the thought-feeling connection for answers.

Hard work has nothing to do with it.

THE FLOW OF ENERGY

While we're on the subject of effort and excellence, let's take a quick detour back to our discussion about passion. I insisted that passion comes from the inside, that one's get-up-and-go is impervious to circumstance. Now I want to talk specifically about what powers that internal passion. (I mean, we don't plug ourselves in at night like an electric car, do we?)

Some people, me included, believe that there's a spiritual flow of energy that runs through, and is common to, all human beings. It's this spiritual flow of energy that stimulates our heartbeats, for example.

Many of the same people also believe that when this energy is flowing freely, human beings feel passionate, open, understanding, and loving. And when this energy is blocked, we feel lethargic, closed off, judgmental, and insecure. What often gets confusing, however, is what regulates this flow of energy (and our feelings) in the first place.

Most point to circumstance or environment. They maintain that what's happening on the outside can affect a person's energy on the inside. We know that's not the case. Another explanation often cited is a physical one: the alignment of the spine and the workings of the central nervous system. This does seem logical. If your body is out of structural alignment, then energy flow—and the body's ability to heal—will be compromised.

But there's also an invisible element at work behind the scenes, overlooked by most of us, that's more capable of restricting this natural flow of energy: a person's thinking.

When your mind is filled with thinking, you leave little room for this spiritual energy to work its way in and then through the system. That's why when you have a lot of noise in your head, you feel listless, and when your head is clear, you feel passionate. And don't forget: It doesn't matter what types of thoughts a person is having. Think twenty-five positive, or even loving, thoughts right now and I guarantee you'll feel exhausted.

So, then, assuming that the aforementioned chain of events is correct, what action can you take at those moments when you lack drive because your thinking is blocking this omnipresent spiritual energy?

None. The answer, as we've seen, comes down to understanding. We begin as a clean slate. Nobody is born with a bunch of stale thinking upstairs. Thinking accumulates over time because we continually make the mistake of trying to fix how we feel. (Doing this requires more and more thought, so we feel more and more sluggish.) But it's not necessary to fix how we feel. It's only necessary to understand that this spiritual energy is always at work, boosting our innate ability to self-correct to clarity.

An omnipresent flow of energy may seem like an odd idea. But what's become more obvious to me each day is that overcoming a lack of passion, or any bad feeling, is as simple as permitting this natural force to do its thing. It's hard to deny that there's something out there that powers our existence and allows us to effortlessly find new perspectives on circumstances that once seemed troubling. My question to you is: Why not take advantage of it to the fullest?

INEXPLICABLE CALM = SUREFIRE SUCCESS

It's not surprising that one of the most harmful symptoms of not allowing one's bound-up feeling state to shift naturally is stress. Have you ever noticed that the most anxious people are the ones who work the hardest to fend off anxiety? They search all over the place for ways to build up their tolerance to stress, when they should be looking within to the spiritual energy that powers their ability to find clarity and calm (the no-resistance way to uproot anxiety).

It's like the well-meaning friend who, when you feel anxious, says, "Just try to relax. Chill and you'll be fine." You could be thinking about anything—a presentation at work, a medical procedure, or even a personal situation. You do your best to relax or stop thinking about the situation, but the harder you try, the worse you end up feeling.

Let's go back to the NFL's Player Protect program discussed in chapter 1. Do you recall how these types of outside-in methods do the opposite of what they set out to do? They point players away from the self-corrective savvy of their own minds. It works the same when you try to relax.

Trying to relax because of something external makes you a victim of your thoughts—about something external.

For instance, let's say you and a buddy are playing golf. You're about to hit a shot when your buddy yells out, "Watch out for the lake over there." You hadn't noticed the lake, but now you can't stop thinking about it, and you're mad at your friend for bringing it up. You try to think about something else, like the flag you're supposed to aim at, but it doesn't work. Now all you see is the lake (and you're getting madder). You swing and . . . you guessed it—kerplunk.

It all comes down to your feelings. No one can make sound judgments and adjustments from a low feeling state. In truth, your agitation on the golf course was an intuitive sign that your thinking was off course (no pun intended) and should not be trusted. If your thinking were on course, you wouldn't feel uptight, insecure, or mad.

Knowing this, by the way, doesn't mean that your head will instantly clear and your golf game improve. It means that you won't attribute your low feelings to something outside of you—your buddy's comment or the lake that just ate your golf ball—so you won't add more thought into your revved-up head. And then you'll be on your way to self-correcting and feeling better, not worse.

That's the reason most forms of therapy, including sports psychology, do not work. They are fact-finding missions designed to expose the circumstantial excuses for a person's unrest. Embark on one of these missions and you might look outside for years—which is what happens to people who stay in therapy indefinitely. When you look inside to your thinking, however, you find inexplicable calm and surefire success.

Last year, I received the following e-mail from Phil Hughes. Phil is an oil executive who, like Maria Venegas, read *Stillpower* and found its paradigm intriguing. So he reached out to me to learn more. The e-mail came on the heels of a conversation we had about two weeks prior. (I've removed some, but not all, of the pleasantries. Aside from being a sharp executive, Phil is a very nice guy.)

Hey Garret,

I have a personal tale I want to tell you about.

Recently, I was at a leadership conference where everyone took a turn presenting to the group. On the morning of my turn, I woke up not feeling right. I was nervous, which was strange because I've given speeches before and consider myself to be good at public speaking.

Fortunately, I knew what my feelings were telling me: that my thinking was off base. I re-minded myself that, if I left it alone, my state of mind was bound to clear. I went off to the con-ference with no expectation as to how I would feel or perform.

Sure enough, my well-being started to rise.

That morning, the group was split into two, and our group had a session on managing change, which engaged me so completely that, immediately, I asked to present the recap when we reconvened with the others.

I had prepared nothing for the presentation. I had two flip-chart pages of notes and a couple of posters to use, but I was so lost in the moment that I barely referred to them. Two or three illustrative and amusing anecdotes had been recounted in our session; I was able to repeat these anecdotes word for word in my presentation with barely a thought, my recall of what had happened and what was said being so total.

The feedback I got on the presentation was nothing but brilliant. Many of my colleagues mentioned that I was a "charismatic presenter." And in truth, I had done nothing that textbooks would have you do. I did not practice; I did not toil over material or what I was going to say. I did not even think. I was so completely engaged that the experience just flowed. I was going to write that I let it flow, but that would have been wrong because there was no conscious effort on my part. It was an out-of-body experience.

And a fantastic testimony to the power of the inside-out approach you teach. I remind myself of this approach whenever my feelings cry out for me to let things be. The benefits of what you share are truly powerful.

All the best,
Phil Hughes

Here are the significant insights from Phil's e-mail about the no-resistance path to excellence: First, your feelings have one purpose; they're your intuitive guide. Second, if left alone, nervous thoughts cannot hinder performance. Third, it's okay to prepare for a performance, but never at the risk of contaminating your instincts. Last, labeling yourself (as a good speaker, in Phil's case) is something that you might want to reconsider.

As a matter of fact, self-labeling is a stifling habit that many of us engage in, without even knowing it. That's why it's important to examine this habit next.

WHY SELF-LABELING IS SELF-DEFEATING

Self-labeling is about as outside-in as it gets. It occurs when we don't listen to our insecure feelings.

Have you ever labeled yourself? You know, "I'm the kind of person who does what I *say* I'm going to do." Or, "When I was young, a specialist told me that I had attention deficit disorder, and to this day I have trouble concentrating." Or, using the rowing machine example, "I stink at rowing. Every time I get on one of those machines I struggle." Or, the staple of twelve-step programs, "My name is so-and-so, and I'm an addict."

I do the same thing. Every now and then, I scam myself into believing my feelings are based on something other than my current thinking—something from the past. When I was thirteen, for example, I witnessed a dreadful incident that fractured my family. So today, I often attribute my desire for and commitment to a cohesive family life to this past adversity. It's normal to do this, but not helpful.

Why is it not helpful? You and I both know the answer: Only my thinking creates my feelings. When my thinking is clear, I feel loving and loyal toward my family. When my thinking is cluttered, I put this loyalty to the test. Therefore, though it may sound counterintuitive, I remain committed to Liz because when I don't feel loving and loyal, I know this feeling comes from me. I don't form an imaginary circumstance-feeling link by looking outside to what Liz says or does, to my past, or to an arbitrary label (I'm a loyal guy) that I've attached to myself.

In fact, labeling your own character accomplishes only one thing—it reinforces insecurity. Yes, it's normal to get confused into believing that your feelings are caused by a circumstance outside. But when you label yourself according to this confusion, you box yourself into artificial judgments and expectations that are virtually impossible to live up to.

The same applies to this poignant example revolving

around family: I once met with a gentleman who had lost his wife a couple of years prior. He was depressed. In his mind the only rationalization for this feeling was the loss of his wife since, according to him, he had been an optimistic person before her passing. Yet, when I made it clear that human beings create all perceptions—including perceptions of themselves—from the inside-out, his opinion shifted.

He said, "Golly, you're right. Sometimes I think about my wife and feel good and sometimes I feel miserable." He went on to realize, "Come to think of it, I've always seen the world that way (from the inside-out). I guess my viewpoint on life, including my wife's passing, is kind of random."

Exactly. Since self-labeling shrinks awareness, limits possibilities, and promotes self-doubt, his portrayal of himself (as being optimistic before his wife's death) was restricting his instinctive ability to find meaning and move forward.

————

No matter what you're up against, even tragedy, you're built to overcome. Just as your body temperature defaults to 98.6 degrees, your mind defaults to consciousness. But, like the other external vices we've covered in this book, self-labeling will always impede this process.

What I hope you now see is that when you're at an elevated level of consciousness, options become visible, so limiting yourself is the last thing you would consider. It's when you naturally fall out of this perspective that your feelings are telling you, "Don't believe what you think." Boundaries are always self-created.

Here's a final and personal take on self-labeling. In the past, one of my boundaries was that I labeled myself as someone who loved to play golf. I'm still fond of the game. But back then, I convinced myself that golf was an important part of my life and it made me happy. I even competed, with success. However, the insightful moment I discovered that my happiness had nothing to do with golf, I immediately stopped spending so much time practicing and playing at the expense of other possibilities and passions. Options for my future then opened up. I became true to myself.

Oh, and another perk: When I do play golf today, I usually play better than I used to—with ease. Go figure.

REMAINING TRUE

Do you know a key reason why authors, teachers, coaches, employers, and parents often fail to get their message across? It's because they cheapen it; they sacrifice; they play to their audience. It's extremely common for people to look toward the world outside, and not to their feelings, when planning their next move. And when they do, their message gets muddled.

Here are two unrelated illustrations of not being true to oneself and sending unclear messages: As you probably know, online blogs and magazines are big business today. So it's customary for writers to create catchy titles for their articles. The title is meant to draw the audience in—whether it truly describes the article's substance or not. Likewise, many parents and coaches exhort clean living to their teenagers or players, only to do the opposite behind closed doors.

Now right off, I'm not saying that people should or shouldn't act a certain way; their behavior is up to them. I'm going to talk about why disingenuousness occurs and what you must understand to avoid the temptation.

Let's be frank. At times, we all look for shortcuts; we're tempted to stretch the truth. Why? Because we attribute our feelings to our circumstances.

Say, using the catchy-title example, an online magazine editor feels pressure to create a viral piece that gets lots of clicks and shares, sells more ad space, and makes the publisher happy. There's nothing abnormal about that. But if the editor doesn't understand that the pressure she feels comes from inside of her—and signifies a passing lack of clarity—she'll fall prey to these feelings and act on the compulsion to do whatever she deems necessary to generate immediate sales. When she acts without clarity, and chooses a misleading title, she runs the risk of alienating her readership and decreases her chances for long-term success.

Two-faced parents and coaches are no different. They encourage their children or players to "look before they leap" and then, when they buy into their own insecure thinking, fail to follow this advice in their own lives.

But here's an unexpected twist: In many cases, the magazine reader, teenager, or athlete won't initially take in the discrepancy that I just pointed out. They'll read the article without grasping that its title doesn't fit, or they'll have no clue about their parents' or coaches' real conduct.

So, why does remaining true even matter?

It matters because those who hype a disingenuous message aren't capable of making an enduring impact. If during one of my talks, for instance, I make statements that aren't sincere, the audience will eventually tune into my hypocrisy, and I'll fail to make a deep-seated connection. Even the good ideas in my message will ultimately get lost.

Reflect for a second. We all know people who once made outwardly impressive short-term gains, only to fall flat on their face since their message wasn't genuine.

I'll say it again and again: It always comes down to what your feelings are trying to say. Thinking insincere thoughts doesn't make you an insincere person; it only makes you *feel* that way. And when you feel that way, I guarantee you won't feel better if you carry those thoughts to fruition. Every mistake you or I have ever made was caused by acting or speaking when our sentiments were telling us, "You know better!"

Like I said in chapter 2, having a thought doesn't mean that the thought is accurate. In fact, the thought itself means nothing. To remain true to yourself, avoid hypocritical behavior, and make long-term gains—follow your feelings. They are foolproof.

A FINAL WORD ON FEELINGS

Feelings. A word that you most likely thought was relegated to the touchy-feely section of your life playbook actually belongs front and center.

How about that?

Indisputably, feelings are your most reliable resource. Nothing or no one can influence how you feel; your feelings come from you.

The thought-feeling connection is the building block of the human experience. I hope that, from the first three chapters of this book, this principle is now clear. What this means is that your feelings are the sole indicator of the competence of your thinking.

When you feel "off" in your gut, it's an indication that you're not thinking straight. You're blocking the omnipresent flow of energy that's designed to return you to clarity. When you feel light or free in your gut, it's an indication that you are thinking straight. Your mind is uncluttered. Because you, like all human beings, cannot control the thoughts that pop into your head, your feelings serve as the middleman between your thoughts and if you should act on your thoughts (your behavior). That is, your feelings tell you if your thinking has merit, or not; if you're on the right path—the path of no resistance—or not.

For example, what should you do if you have the thought that you should quit your well-paying desk job of twenty years? Listen to your feelings; they'll guide your next move. If you feel bound up, your feelings are telling you to get to your desk and go back to work. If it was truly time to leave your job, you might feel melancholy, but you wouldn't feel bound up. Knowing that you feel your thinking, not your circumstance (your job), prevents you from acting on potentially detrimental thoughts. It allows you to self-correct back to coherence.

With this in mind, I want to close this chapter by examining a more delicate scenario: what can happen when people numb or anesthetize their feelings, predominantly through the use of drugs and alcohol. Many will disagree with what I'm about to say, and that's fine. As we discussed, I can only speak based on my own level of consciousness. So from my heart, this is what I see.

Say a young man who doesn't understand the thought-feeling connection has been experiencing a rash of destructive thoughts and feelings. Regrettably, since we live in a mostly outside-in world, no one informs the young man that he feels his thinking. Convinced that his feelings are coming from something outside of him, he delves into his life for the causes of why he feels this way. He examines his childhood, his surroundings, a genetic diagnosis, and his seemingly grim future. He's looking into a bottomless pit. His thoughts spiral downward and more out of control. It gets so bad that he turns to drugs or the abuse of alcohol to suppress his anxious feeling state—a last resort.

As a result of the narcotic, the young man feels calmer, more in command. But since his feelings don't create his thinking (thinking always comes first), he's still experiencing an onslaught of destructive thoughts. Now the middleman is gone. The link from his thoughts to his feelings has been breached by an outside numbing agent. There's no way for him to know that his destructive thoughts have no merit. He accepts them as real. He acts on these thoughts, with perilous consequence.

The purpose of this example is not to excuse dysfunctional behavior or to paint a defeatist picture of the world in which we live. Not at all. The purpose of this example, like the purpose of this book, is to provide a promising direction not yet considered.

The unseen factor behind *any* type of dysfunction is how much thinking a person is carrying around in his or her head at any given moment. That's why it doesn't help to give people things to do, or have them analyze past circumstances, when they are struggling. More thinking leads to more confusion, which leads to more dysfunction.

Rather, everyone must learn that painful feelings—insecurity, judgment, rage—are created and held in place via thought, not by anything that happens on the outside. Once this principle is understood, the accumulation of old thinking begins to fall away on its own and is replaced with insight and wisdom (new thought). Then feelings improve and behavior turns productive.

At this point in *The Path of No Resistance*, my suggestion, especially for young people, is this: Listen to your feelings. Don't deaden them by looking outside for answers or justifications (adding thought). Life is a roller coaster of never-ending experiences and opportunities. If you start messing with the thought-feeling connection, you'll obstruct your innate ability to rise to the top.

Here's a quick half-time overview of the material we've covered so far:

- You live in the feeling of your thinking—not the feeling of your circumstances.

- Your reality is created from the inside-out via your thinking.

- Your feelings are your guide to the reliability of your thinking. A bound-up gut feeling means that your thinking and reality in the moment aren't reliable.

So, what comes next? To keep your self-correcting system working to full capacity, you must stay in the game. I'll cover that in chapter 4.

4.

STAYING IN THE GAME

"With patient and firm determination, we will press on until every valley of despair is exalted to new peaks of hope; until every mountain of pride and irrationality is made low by the leveling process of humility and compassion; until the rough places of injustice are transformed into a smooth plane of equality of opportunity; and until the crooked places of prejudice are transformed by the straightening process of bright-eyed wisdom."[8]

—*Dr. Martin Luther King Jr.*

If the mind is naturally resilient, what should we do when we feel bad and despair just won't exit? Should we sit still and wait for our troubles to pass? Do we really get used to certain life events, as many suggest?

Most of us believe that when something disturbing happens, the passage of time is what erases the hurt. But take

---

8. Martin Luther King Jr., "The Quest for Peace and Justice" (Nobel Lecture, University of Oslo, December 11, 1964).

a closer look. Some people obsess for years over the same thought about the same circumstance without finding a solution. And everyone gets stuck for longer than they'd prefer. Can it really be time that heals all wounds?

No. Regardless of how much time goes by or how still we sit, when we nourish old ways of thinking (wounds) with belief, those wounds tend to hang around and multiply. We all do it, sometimes for seconds and sometimes for years. Recall, though, that the magic bullet is to listen to your feelings. They point you away from paralysis by analysis, the mental activity that holds errant thinking in place. But did you know that your feelings serve a paradoxical purpose as well? They point you away from the *physical inactivity* that can also jam your thought system.

This principle is at the crux of "staying in the game."

Dr. Martin Luther King Jr. became one of the preeminent change agents the world has ever known because he stayed in the game. During Dr. King's fight for the most moral of causes, he knew that his ups and downs (his feelings) were the result of the turbulence of his own thinking—not the turbulence of the world in which he lived. Knowing this provided Dr. King with the fortitude to remain on course (stay in the game) and lead with the clearest of heads—no matter the behavior of those who opposed his message.

Here's a basic example of staying in the game that might apply to you. Suppose you're a businessperson who's about to pitch a new client and you feel nervous—real "off" in your gut. As it was for Dr. King, what you need to know is that your bad feelings are not instructing you to ponder or alter your game plan. Your feelings are pointing you to clarity of thought by telling you to stay in the game and get *on* with your game plan. If you were supposed to pull back, there wouldn't be any bad feelings; pulling back would be instinctive and immediate. No thought involved at all.

Here's another example. In October 2012, my area got nailed by one of the worst storms to ever hit the East Coast of the United States: Hurricane Sandy. Our New Jersey home was spared, but sadly our property lost many old trees. So the views from our house and patio became significantly different. In the storm's immediate aftermath, it made sense, to me, to spend whatever time and money necessary to replace the foliage that we lost. I even considered hiring a high-priced landscape architect to draw up plans and recommend the right replacement trees and contractors. Fact is: I felt upset, insecure, and analytical; nearly desperate.

Why did I feel this way? Because I attached my feelings to something outside of me—what Hurricane Sandy had done to my property. I wanted it put back to the way it was before. I was also on the brink of spending a lot of time, money, and effort on what should not have been a priority.

What I decided to do, instead, was stay in the game. Even though I felt upset and insecure, I helped my neighbors and friends. I wrote articles about my hurricane experience, hoping they might do some good. I supported my family.

Before I knew it, my bound-up feelings had vanished. I forgot about the trees, and, better yet, now that the dust has settled, I love our new views from the house and patio![9]

Quite simply: Your mind is always working in your favor—if you keep out of its way. When you recognize what your insecure feelings are trying to tell you, turn your back on circumstance, and just go about your business (whatever that may be), your blemished thinking will fade, allowing new outlooks to easily appear.

So a good measuring stick for when you should sit back, or when you should roll up your sleeves and go for it, is how much mental energy you're expending in the moment. Holing yourself up in the house and rummaging for answers, like I did at first with the tree issue, is exhausting. But staying in the game, like I did when I chose to help others, guides you away from attaching feelings to circumstance. It frees and calms you.

As with any behavior, it never matters whether you're sitting still or running here and there. What matters is the mind-set from which you're sitting or running. People who understand that they live in the feeling of their thinking, and that their feelings and thinking will always improve naturally, conserve energy regardless of what they're doing. They also have a knack for overcoming "hurricanes."

---

9. We'll see some other cool revelations that occurred during Hurricane Sandy in chapter 5.

Like me, you've probably spun your wheels a time or two. But, as you'll see in this chapter, it takes a lot more energy to judge something or someone, hunt down tranquility, or rack your brain for answers than it does to just get on with life. The most draining thing a person can ever do is look outside to explain his or her feelings.

THE ART OF SHOWING UP

In chapter 3, I said that Syd Banks claimed that wisdom is everywhere. Here's evidence. Writer, actor, and director Woody Allen once said, "Showing up is 80 percent of life."[10] Indeed, if we let grass grow under our feet, opportunity might pass us by. But when we choose to show up for work, a class, or a training session, we put ourselves in a position for consciousness and success to collide.

After I coined the word "stillpower" and wrote a book about it, I found that many people assumed I was promoting the act of remaining still (rather than the power of a still mind-set) in order to find excellence. I remember one client asked me, "Are you saying that it's best to sit on the sidelines and wait for things to clear when I'm in a low state of mind?" Not for a second.

Let's say you're a boxer, and you're training for a fight.

---

10. Susan Braudy, "He's Woody Allen's Not-So-Silent Partner," *The New York Times*, August 21, 1977.

Your daily schedule includes some serious training because if you don't train seriously, chances are you'll suffer some physical harm—let alone lose the fight. Yet one morning you wake up with perplexing thoughts: "Should I go to the gym or not?" As confusion reigns, you assume (because of the confusion) that you're better off staying home, even though you still feel uncertain and perhaps guilty, too.

But what if you misread your own feelings? In this book, I've shown how often that takes place. Truth is: When you really need a day off, that notion won't be one bit confusing. That morning you will be so tired that you'll sleep straight through your alarm. You won't have to *think* about what you should or shouldn't do next.

A feeling of uncertainty, therefore, is a sign that you ought to show up; you need to get out of bed and into the gym; you must stay in the game. Your thinking—not your training—is getting in your way at that moment. No matter the situation, you're better off carrying on in the midst of chaotic thoughts since, when they occur, you're temporarily unequipped to deviate from your charted course.

Don't forget: Your feelings are your guide. When it's time to change things up, the feeling will be direct, immediate, and resolute (i.e., no thought). When it's time to stay in the game, the feeling will be scattered, confused, and ambivalent (i.e., too much thought).

Here's a different illustration. Most athletes, businesspeople, or doctors with whom I work have fast-paced jobs.

They, too, sometimes get confused about when to draw back and when to go for it. A surgeon might say, "I see what you mean, my feelings are a barometer of my thoughts and mind-set. But I work in an operating room. If I feel rattled, I can't just stop and wait for clarity to show up."

Precisely. Surgeons who understand that they feel their thinking, and not what happens in the operating room, have no reason to stop and wait for clarity. They don't get bogged down by the self-created perceptions that come from a temporarily cluttered mind-set. They keep engaged; they remain resilient; they become clear.

———————

Here's a question you might find revelatory: If you're strolling through a garden and feel insecure, are your insecure feelings coming from the garden?

No. So why do you blame your feelings on other circumstances or environments?

I understand. This paradigm is different—particularly for those of you who believe that something is actually wrong in your life when you don't feel quite right. However, a lack of clarity is never a call to intentionally sit on your hands, take a breather, or chill. A lack of clarity is the normal byproduct of the fact that you think. *There is nothing broken.* And that's all you need to know to keep strolling (through a garden or anywhere) and allow your psychological immune system to return you to balance.

As I told you at the beginning of *The Path of No Resistance*, don't fret if this paradigm doesn't make perfect sense right now. Just stay in the game with me; let's explore a little deeper. You never know. Your mind just might clear before we finish this chapter.

GET TO WORK AND DIAL IT DOWN

This past spring, a baseball-playing client sent me a text message. The sit-on-your-hands/stay-in-the-game dichotomy was new and unusual to him. It was also still fuzzy. He had gone 0 for 4 in a game that night and wanted my opinion on whether or not he should immediately hit the batting cage to work out the kinks in his swing. I answered him with a question, "How are you feeling right now?"

His response: "I'm definitely not happy about my performance today, but I'm doing okay. I'm open, enthused, and determined to discover what I'm doing wrong."

"Well," I said, "it's not really my role to tell you what to do, but if you're asking: Get to work!"

About a month later, the same player sent me a text message about a slightly different predicament. Even though his batting average had improved since our last exchange, on that night he had struggled—again going 0 for 4. I asked the same question, "How are you feeling right now?"

His response: "I guess I'm okay, but my teammates and I were on our way to dinner and I got this strange insecure feeling that I should stay behind and work on my swing. Now, I'm totally confused about whether I should hit the cage or not."

"Go have a nice dinner," I replied. "The last place you should be right now is in the batting cage."

My reasoning in both instances, of course, had nothing to do with the player's performance (0 for 4).

Think back to my college hockey coach, Coach Batt. Unlike him and many who would prescribe a "nose to the grindstone" to fix current flaws, I believe a person's ability to correct bad habits is based on his or her level of clarity and consciousness at that particular moment—which will always occur independent of circumstance.

In other words, staying in the game has nothing to do with behavior. It has to do with whether or not you listen to what your feelings are trying to say. During our first conversation, my client immediately figured that the batting cage was calling him. His thinking just got in the way. So I pointed him back inward—toward his open, enthused, and determined feelings. During our second conversation, his instinct (to go to dinner) was on target, too; it again was just momentarily halted by his thinking. In this case, staying in the game actually meant dialing it down and enjoying some time with his teammates.

That's just it. The time to dial it down is when dialing it down just happens. The time to stay in the game is when thoughts about doing anything cause uncertainty or anxiousness. Truth be told, throughout the course of writing this book, I've had moments of procrastination (yet I stayed in the game) and moments when I intentionally and profitably kept away from my writing (another form of staying in the game).

Sometimes pulling back is necessary. Sometimes we forget that it's not the job or chore we feel—it's our thinking—so we drag our feet and make excuses about it. Being productive is always about looking inside. Because no matter what we do, being productive doesn't occur when we stop and think. It occurs on its own.

THE NATURE OF PRODUCTIVITY

Evidently, the thought-feeling link is relevant to everything. Productivity included.

Most performance and business experts, though, don't see it that way. There are thousands of how-to-be-productive books on the market today. No matter how well thought out or helpful some may appear, in my experience nearly all of them lack enduring advice. Reason being, they take the fact that you feel your thinking and not your circumstances totally out of the equation.[11]

Oh, these books tell you what to think and do in order to

---

11. Here's a book about productivity, among other things, and the principle of thought: Jamie Smart, *Clarity: Clear Mind, Better Performance, Bigger Results* (West Sussex, UK: Capstone, 2013).

excel. They also infer that if you don't get the job done right, your state of mind will fall to pieces, so you'd better adopt the strategy they're promoting, ASAP!

Ugh. A lack of productivity is a symptom of an inefficient mind-set; it's not the cause of it. By recommending external tactics to become industrious, these experts have put the cart way in front of the horse.

So, let's turn the nature of productivity back to its true self. Specifically to a question you should answer before considering ways to improve productivity at work, at home, in the classroom, or on the field: What can I do to clear my mind in order to kick some butt?

The answer, as you might have figured, is nothing. You need to stay in the game—leave ill-at-ease thinking alone—and you'll easily return to your most productive psychological perspective. It's when you try to fix a lull in productivity that it becomes a crapshoot. As I've said, do anything from an inefficient mind-set and your performance level goes south.

An associate of mine, Tim Grahl, once put my perspective on productivity to the test. Tim's company, Out:think Group, is a cutting-edge resource for authors and speakers. Tim is a super-creative guy. He and I have spent many hours talking about the fallacy of productivity books, and the necessity of not trying to force efficiency through the use of another person's theories or strategies.

So, when a usual Monday morning rolled around and

Tim experienced unusual negative thoughts about his to-do list, followed by anxious feelings, followed by the temptation to take a break from his work even before starting, he decided to stay in the game. Not by reaching for a productivity strategy to pump himself up. Not by pulling back. He decided to allow his negative thoughts to settle and his level of clarity to rise on its own. What exactly did Tim do? He poured himself into his to-do list.

And the result? Tim easily completed all of his tasks by lunch, so he had the afternoon open to ardently start a new project—for me, I might add.

From my frame of reference, it seems like most business writers and performance coaches today are pulling productivity strategies out of thin air. If you take someone else's method for finding excellence and mix it with your own inner wisdom and instincts, what you get is a flare-up of confusion and uncertainty, never lasting success.

Incidentally, not all business writers are missing it these days. I'll talk about one at the end of this chapter who makes a lot of sense.

In the interim, if you seek a high level of performance, but just can't get out of your own way, consider these seven fundamental productivity reminders. They'll direct you inward, where your ability to stay in the game and your most productive self rest.

1. Your opportunity to be productive is only as good as your thinking and mind-set in the moment.

2. Any productivity strategy will be ineffective from an unclear mental perspective.

3. If you stay on task, your level of clarity and productivity will improve on their own.

4. If you're wondering whether or not it's time to take a break, it's not time.

5. If taking a break is automatic and obvious—instinctual—take it. You won't need me to remind you of this, however.

6. Your perception of a task is based on your level of clarity in the moment. The same task will appear challenging from an unclear mind-set, and a piece of cake from a clear one.

7. No matter what you do, acting from inspiration is productive. Acting from desperation is not.

WOODS, COLVIN, AND GLADWELL

Here, near the middle of chapter 4, let's regroup. I've talked a lot about what staying in the game is, and I've talked about its link to productivity, but I feel it's equally important to talk about what staying in the game is not.

Staying in the game is not the theory of "deliberate practice" that Geoff Colvin reveals in his book *Talent Is Overrated*.[12] It's also not applying the ten-thousand-hour rule (i.e., greatness requires practicing a specific task for ten thousand hours) popularized in Malcolm Gladwell's book *Outliers: The Story of Success*.[13] As we have seen in this book, it's never the amount of time put in or how hard you push that determines excellence—it's the mind-set from which you do the pushing. To be blunt, staying in the game is the opposite of grinding your rear end off!

I respect the work of these two fine authors; we just see the source of success differently. And since many people are turning to information, supposition, and data in books like these for motivation, I think it's important to highlight this difference.

In brief, it's outside-in versus inside-out. To me, there's not a cause-and-effect relationship between maximizing talent and how long or hard one works. The data shows a correlation, but that's all it shows (more on data and correlations shortly).

In *Talent Is Overrated*, Colvin uses golfer Tiger Woods as proof for his theory. He insists that Woods's golf mastery was the result of hours and hours of rigorous practice.

12. Geoff Colvin, *Talent Is Overrated: What Really Separates World-Class Performers from Everybody Else* (New York: Portfolio, 2008).

13. Malcolm Gladwell, *Outliers: The Story of Success* (New York: Little, Brown and Company, 2008).

Really? The fact is that Woods still puts in tons of practice today. His level of achievement, though, is not what it used to be. If his work ethic was responsible for his mastery and success, why isn't Woods winning at the same rate now as he once did?

Some say it's because years of training have taken their toll on his body. Many say his personal issues off the course are insurmountable. The former might be true; the latter is not. Either way, don't forget that Woods won the 2008 US Open while playing on a broken leg, and amid the constant scrutiny of his behavior, he has continued his quest to be the best golfer of all time.

So, if it's not lack of effort, injury, or living in the public eye, what's stopping Woods from experiencing his former level of success?

Simple. It's the extent to which Woods stays in the game.

As it works for everyone, when Woods's feelings falter, his perceptual field narrows as awareness descends. There's not much he can do to prevent this, but hitting a wayward golf shot should be the worst result. However, if he overlooks that his low feelings come from the normal ebb and flow of thought, and tries to make adjustments to his swing or his life in the hope of feeling better, things will nosedive. Staying in the game means that Woods should go about his business and not fix things—since if left alone, his thinking and feelings are destined to clear. Staying in the game is the opposite of panic. Staying in the game is faith. Staying in the game means that one's instinctual ability to make corrections is about to return.

What staying in the game is not is going to the practice range and pounding golf balls from a state of mind that's guaranteed to take one's performance lower. Colvin talks about the fact that Woods and his father both defined "hard work" as the foundation of their success. It might have looked that way to them, but remember, passion is not the same thing as hard work. (As Woods has also mentioned, when he was young, he could hit golf balls and train all day without the slightest sense of exertion.)

Finally, the most dangerous part of the theories of deliberate practice and the ten-thousand-hour rule that Colvin and Gladwell purport, respectively, is not the impact they have on professional athletes like Woods. It's that these theories run the risk of revving up the brains and bodies of our young people. I've worked with high school and college students whose parents have used Colvin's and Gladwell's theories as justification for pushing their sons and daughters *way too hard.*

As I often say to parents: "A child's or anyone's level of consciousness, or state of mind, must always be the number-one priority before the start of any task, endeavor, or exercise."

YOUR NEVER-ENDING (AND NEEDLESS)
PURSUIT OF THE ZONE

An interesting thing about the strategies of both deliberate practice and the hours-applied rule is that they're redundant. From freedom and ease, everyone knows how hard to push and how much time is needed to become proficient or even great at something. From a bound-up mental state, the best anyone can hope for is mediocrity.

Again, this type of wisdom is not imparted from the outside. In their books, Colvin and Gladwell present data, scientific studies, and fact-based cases; they theorize that through tons of hard (and painful) practice *anyone* can excel. But these are just theories and fallible ones. They're untrue because those who apply them don't always achieve greatness.

One of my mentors, George Pransky, once said, "Spun correctly, data proves that storm-sewer overflow causes umbrella usage." George's comment may sound silly, but it does show that correlations—whether we're talking about a correlation between storm-sewer overflow and umbrella usage or between deliberate practice/hours applied and mastery—are not always cause and effect. See what I mean about theories backed by data?

The fact is that we're besieged by the information and opinions of people who are doing the best they can from their current level of consciousness, or understanding of how the mind functions. I suppose the same could be said of me, though my purpose is to teach you *how the system works*—not to tell you *what to do with the system*. If you take from this book that behavioral theories and strategies are not the ultimate answer, and nothing else, then I've done a decent job. Behavior is after-the-fact—the damage has already been done.

Think of it this way: Follow someone else's advice and, with your free will and instincts weakened, you won't be capable of doing anything right. Look inward to the fact that you feel your thinking, and you won't be capable of doing anything wrong. Looking inward is staying in the game. It's what allows your mind to default to clarity, wonder, and rewarding behavior.

How about you? When you picked up this book, were you hoping to find clear-cut steps to help change your life? A beeline to the zone? A blueprint for excellence? Well, I'm here to tell you that they won't be found in a book. And it doesn't matter anyway—you don't *have* to be in a perfect mind-set to perform at the top of your game. There's never a need to pursue the zone.

Relieved? I hope so, because only when your mind is free from the burden of trying to find mental clarity does it leave space for insights and excellence to come pouring in. To be honest, I'm not a big fan of the term "the zone" anyway.

Here's another illustration of what can happen if you follow another person's advice or techniques in order to find psychological perfection: Let's say you're a pro golfer playing in the last group of the last round of a major championship. The night before, you tossed and turned, and now on your way to the course, your anxious thoughts and feelings won't let up. You're also convinced (like most people) that anxious thoughts and feelings represent a problem; you believe that you must be in the zone to win a major championship.

So, you recall a deep-breathing/visualization technique that your sports psychologist recommended for these exact moments. You think about how you're supposed to apply the technique: "Okay, breathe in through the nose, out through the mouth, and picture the ball going toward the target." But then you think, "Oh, wait, maybe it's breathe in through the mouth, out through the nose, and picture myself holding the championship trophy. Darn, I can't remember what to do. I better figure something out, and quick!"

What's happened is that your revved-up thinking and anxiety have generated more revved-up thinking and anxiety. You've crammed your head with deliberate thought, leaving no room for fresh ideas to work their way in. Said differently, since you didn't know that clarity of mind is guaranteed to appear on its own, you jammed the inherent functioning of the system.

But what's the alternative? What should you do when, prior to "big" performances, you're feeling unsure or anxious? What should you do when you're not in the zone?

You know the answer. The same thing Tim Grahl did

when he felt unproductive about his to-do list, the same thing our baseball player did when he felt insecure about his swing, and the same thing I did during the writing of this book when I felt stuck—stay in the gosh-darn game! Syd Banks called feelings our virus detectors. They're pointing us inside to a temporary virus of thought—not outside to doing something to overcome a bothersome to-do list, a finicky swing, or the annoyance of writer's block.

And just so we're crystal clear, looking within, or staying in the game, is the opposite of using a fix-it technique. It's what everyone does instinctively, before our inner wisdom falls prey to the dos and don'ts of others.

———

In chapter 3, I said that mental health, or consciousness, rests within everyone—no matter their current level of well-being. What this means is that you're already living in the zone 24/7. You just don't feel that way because of all the intellectual wrangling going on inside your own head.

Every day, in both my work and personal life, I become more amazed at how easily the human mind will self-correct to clarity and consciousness when we stop getting in the way by trying to fix our thinking. No one can find a good feeling if they plug away from a state of confusion.

That being the case, here are my nine reasons why the harder you try to find the zone (clarity of mind), the further from it you travel:

1. Finding the zone doesn't require that you do something. Clarity of mind is unconditional.

2. Finding the zone is not something you attain—it's your natural state.

3. Using a method to find the zone divorces you from the wisdom within—and your innate ability to self-correct.

4. Being in the zone, or not, has nothing to do with the circumstances of your life.

5. The zone is a state of no thought. Using a strategy to get there requires thought—the exact opposite of what you're looking for.

6. Believing that you have to be in the zone to succeed only energizes a temporarily low mind-set.

7. If you're trying to fix your thoughts in order to get to the zone, then you don't understand how neutral your thoughts actually are.

8. From a low psychological perspective, you're not seeing life clearly, so grinding your way out is a never-ending struggle.

9. Outcomes are not an appraisal of self-worth. So zone or no zone, the opportunity always exists for development, growth, and success.

Do you now see why I'm not a fan of the term "the zone"? Trying to reach it is akin to trying to fall asleep. Sleep happens naturally. Unless, that is, you apply thought and get in your own way. No matter the circumstance or problem, instinctive answers are always right around the corner.

THE PROBLEM-SOLVING FAST TRACK

In virtually every business, school, sporting environment, or family today, people are doing their best to solve problems. And that's admirable. Yet in my opinion, like those trying to find the zone, most are working way harder than they should. Even I make this mistake, at times.

On one such occasion, I absentmindedly scheduled two meetings for the same hour and racked my brain searching for the solution, without success. So I resigned myself to the fact that at least one client was going to be upset with me, possibly two. Funny thing, though, the minute I did this my thinking slowed and the answer to my supposed quandary appeared. Since both clients were members of the same organization, I offered a joint training where insights could be shared freely. It worked, and both clients thanked me for what they learned that day.

Here's the way 99 percent of us approach our problems:

> *We perceive a circumstance as difficult, so we conclude that the way to solve it is to think about it some more.*

Here's the inside-out, stay-in-the-game way to approach our problems:

We perceive a circumstance as difficult, so we conclude that we're not thinking correctly.

That's right. As with every example in *The Path of No Resistance*, to solve a problem, you must understand that problems always exist in your thinking, never in circumstance. From a clear head—a state of fluent thinking— answers and revelations abound. From a cluttered head—a state of overthinking—it's all confusion and roadblocks.

In other words, just because you can't find a solution doesn't mean that one doesn't exist. All of us have experienced struggles that appeared to be the result of a certain situation, only to later ask ourselves: "This situation isn't so complicated. What in the world was troubling me?" In my experience, there's never a causal relationship between how much we struggle and what we're struggling about.

You already know this, but I'm persistent when I want to be, so I'll say it again: Problems are never the cause of a disquiet mind-set; they're a symptom of a disquiet mind-set. When you willfully dig into a perplexing situation, you only exacerbate the distortion that created it. You create your perceptions from in to out, right? That's why it makes little sense to think more about a problem that's the result of a glut of thinking to begin with.

If you're a parent of a teenager, for instance, have you ever tried to help reason your child through a funk only to be blown off completely? That's because most teens know that reasoning through a funk is ineffective. They have an untarnished feel for the true source of their ups and downs: their thinking. Talking about, coping with, or putting a positive spin on something requires additional thought, which leads to more grief—not less.

Last August, I received the following e-mail from master cyclist and super-nice person Deb Visentin. It's a profound example of the difference between thinking into your problems and staying in the game and allowing your troubles to work through on their own. I often describe this difference as wrestling with an experience versus embracing the daylights out of it. After all, the plunge on a roller coaster can be the path of no resistance, if you choose not to fight it.

> Hi Garret,
>
> I just wanted to thank you for sharing *Stillpower* with the world. I am a master cyclist and have competed, with success, at the national and international levels. However, I have increasingly struggled with motivation and self-defeating thought processes.
>
> I now realize that I have been overthinking my problems and my problem-solving approach has been backwards. Essentially, I've been keeping

myself at the low end of the roller coaster, as you might put it. I've read a lot of sports psychology books, tried meditation, affirmations, life-coaching, and hypnosis to improve my self-confidence and approach to competing—all with no luck. I was at my wit's end. I was searching for the secret. Instead of gaining self-confidence, I seemed to be losing my sense of self. Each external strategy would not produce a sustained improvement. They were taxing on me, and only made me more confused and upset. The thought of trying another imagery technique did my head in.

Thankfully, I ran across your book and later your website. Suddenly, the light went on. My wheels had been spinning, and I knew it! With each strategy that I employed, I was getting deeper into uncertainty.

But now, understanding that my mind is designed to become conscious naturally has put the power back with me. Looking inward to my thinking, and not outward, puts me back at the wheel—it feels so right.

I love my sport, I'm good at it, and I'm looking forward to experiencing the passion I felt when I first competed.

I will no longer try to fight myself through any negativity because I know it's temporary. All I need to do is stay in the game and know the roller coaster will soon trend upward. Every day it gets easier, and my time at the low end gets shorter. Simply amazing!

Many, many thanks,
Deb Visentin

The nitty-gritty of problem solving, as revealed in Deb's e-mail, is this: You can't solve problems that would not exist if your thinking were optimal. That's why staying in the game is so vital; it directs you away from trying to make sense of life using Vaseline-smeared glasses. Again, resilience is not found by looking to the world around you to explain and fix your feelings. Doing this stalls your penchant to self-correct and find insightful solutions.

THE POWER OF RECONSIDERING

Here's something else about the faulty habit of looking to the world outside to explain your inner sensations (and thus obstructing your natural resilience): People who look outside tend to be narrow-minded and set in their ways. People who don't are prone to reconsider their opinions and take a broader view.

Where on the spectrum do you fall?

From my perspective, all of us would be better off, achieve more, and the world would be a better place, if we lived closer to the open-minded side. To do so, however, we must understand the illogic in looking to our circumstances for justifications or excuses.

Here's an example of this involving my daughter, Chelsea: One night while in a low mood, I made the mistake of wandering onto one of Chelsea's social media accounts. And, as other parents might relate, I did not like what I saw. I became angry—I mean, really angry. I yelled upstairs to her, "Come down here immediately!" My intention, at first, was to give Chelsea a piece of my mind and demand that she remove some of her online posts. Yet, somewhere between my outburst and her arrival downstairs, something shifted.

It occurred to me: "Now hold on, knucklehead—you see the posts as wrong, but this is clearly not how your sixteen-year-old daughter sees them."

Why did this occur to me? Why did I take a second look at my own perceptions? Because I woke up to the fact that my thinking—not Chelsea's social media posts—formed the basis for my feelings. I reconsidered my point of view. My anger was a vivid reminder that my thinking at that moment was not to be trusted or followed. Holding Chelsea responsible for this feeling inside of me was clearly a step in the wrong direction.

So what happened when Chelsea came downstairs? First, I apologized for screaming. Then we had an enjoyable chat about our different perspectives about social media. We both learned something from the experience. And while I still don't agree with her completely, and vice versa, I know that Chelsea was buoyed by my trust in her. In fact, the next morning I noticed she had made some adjustments to her accounts, including this tweet on Father's Day:

Happy Father's Day to my main man
@GarretKramer. I love you, Daddy!

What more can I say?

The next time you feel angry, uptight, or anxious—please, don't blame it on circumstance. For the umpteenth time, your feelings come from you. Simply grab hold of this principle and see how easy it is to override judgmental dispositions, find inspiration, and uncover a loving outlook on *anything*.

Now that's something for all of us to consider.

WHY FREE WILL AND SUCCESS GO HAND IN HAND

How do you suppose the late South African president Nelson Mandela overcame his personal judgments, found inspiration and love, and survived twenty-seven years of captivity with such dignity and grace? He was cognizant, keenly so, of the path of no resistance. That's how.

Mandela knew that his experience in jail was formulated by his own thinking—not by what anyone did to him. That's not to say that he didn't have feelings of hatred or despair during his imprisonment. I bet he did. But feelings were his virus detector, and he knew that hatred and despair were viruses for sure.

The opposite of exercising free will is believing that something on the outside can regulate your life in any way. Circumstance or environment be damned, Mandela was free. And just like him—in spite of your boss, children, parents, teacher, or coach—you're free to tackle life in any way that *you* see fit. We'll get to rules, expectations, and goals next, but for now understand this: Adhering to a code of conduct (like Mandela did in prison) does not mean that a code of conduct can change the way you think.

Everyone is born with free will—everyone. So why do so many of us forfeit our free will and follow the paths of others? Why do so few of us consistently act from this intrinsic level of functioning?

The answer brings us back to the prevalence of the outside-in paradigm. From the time we're young, we're told to be afraid of this or that; we're taught the difference between right and wrong. We live at the mercy of an illusion: the circumstance-feeling link. For example, young children think nothing of playing outside for hours. No matter the cold or heat, they don't contemplate circumstance. Until, that is, a concerned adult warns them to put on a jacket or drink plenty of fluids.

To be clear, I'm not saying that layering up in the cold or hydrating in the heat isn't essential for kids—it is. My point is that left to their own intuition, there's a good chance that kids will figure this out for themselves. And if they don't, and a nudge in a certain direction is required, don't disregard that kids are allowed to see things differently. The minute a young person's inner wisdom and instincts become shrouded by the opinions or judgments of someone else, his or her free will takes its first hit. When that horse leaves the barn, achievement becomes more and more difficult.

Remember when we talked about productivity strategies and their potential negative effects? Well, a child or anyone who is subject to overbearing superiors or constant hovering will also react negatively. Reason being, the clash between a person's intuition and the perspective of another almost always results in a bound-up mind-set—a level of functioning from which it's impossible to perform.

Consider it like this: How do you feel inside when you're told what to do or how to act? Now try to perform, or make a balanced decision, from that defensive, irritated, or insecure standpoint.

If you're now wondering what can be done about this seesaw battle between providing or receiving loving advice and hindering free will, this is how it looks to me: First, judging another person and holding him or her accountable to an indiscriminate code of conduct won't work in the long term. What will work, in my experience, is pointing others inward to their thinking in order to explain their feelings, and then allowing behavior to fall into place on its own.

Next, all of us—youngsters, pay attention, too—must

come to grips with the fact that most of the time we can't do anything about an authoritarian figure (parent, coach, teacher, or employer). That's why it's essential to know that these individuals have zero control over our feelings. Truth is, when our mental states are low, these individuals will appear tough to deal with. But when our mental states are high, we'll get exactly where they're coming from and find our own way to use or discard their advice.

———————

One last thing before we leave this topic. There's nothing that expresses your free will more fully than turning your back on a circumstance that appears troubling. Your ability to do this, however, always comes down to how vividly you see the role of thought in crafting your perceptions. The deeper you understand that you live in the feeling of your thinking, and not the feeling of your circumstances, the easier it is to stay in the game and exercise your basic right to be free. Keep in mind: People who believe everything they think live in self-created prisons.

Now we're set to continue down this revolutionarily simple path. Next, let's take a close look at the setting of rules, expectations, and goals. It's no mystery that this is one of my biggest instinct-cramping pet peeves.

ARE YOU SETTING RULES, EXPECTATIONS, AND GOALS? HERE'S WHY THEY'RE NOT WORKING

At the summer camp my children attended between the ages of eight and fifteen, counselors made a concerted effort to eliminate bullying, mischief, and other forms of rebellious behavior. The camp owner and management team even decided to promote their camp as an environment where meanness has no place. As such, right before the summer of 2012, they required all campers and parents to sign a code-of-conduct agreement, which listed twenty-two camper expectations in detail.

Seems reasonable and responsible, right?

But here's the result: Behavior at this camp did not improve—in fact, it got worse. That summer, several campers were repeatedly disciplined for their unruly actions. They were made to scrub dishes in the kitchen and fold clothes in the laundry. At camp, mind you!

This situation, I lament, is comparable to what's happening on college campuses around the world where underage students are abusing alcohol at alarming rates. The typical university response to this dilemma is to set more stringent expectations and throw more rules at the student population, even though as guidelines grow, behavior continues to falter. It's the same predicament I revealed in chapter 1 in regard to pro sports. Even with increasingly intense player-development strategies, goal-oriented approaches, and the specter of fines and suspensions, the number of dysfunctional actions among professional athletes is escalating by the day, both on and off the playing field.

Enough is enough. How much more proof do we need that managing behavior—including setting expectations, rules, and goals—does not inhibit poor behavior? (It doesn't lead to success either, which we'll dig into in a minute.) Poor behavior is a symptom. Not knowing where feelings come from is the cause.

But what's the answer? Why is this trend occurring? If setting stricter standards doesn't work, what can be done to eliminate hurtful and disruptive conduct?

The answers revolve around a person's free will and what happens when this innate attribute is compromised. To me, there's no doubt: In setting expectations, leaders today are energizing the behavior they're trying to deter in the first place. Anytime you tell someone what to do, you undermine that person's instincts.

To illustrate, if I tell one of my sons how I think he should behave when he's away at college, my expectations are bound to clash with *his* definition of right and wrong. This will result in the opposite of a clear head when he finds himself in an unfamiliar situation—a fraternity party, a difference of opinion with a professor, or even competing for a starting spot on the baseball team. And you know where a lack of clarity can lead.

In other words, when we fill people's heads with warnings

or things to watch out for, we give them more to think about, and nothing good comes from an excess of thought.

Staying in the game and allowing one's psychological immune system to respond is a whole lot simpler. That's why, to me, we must start pointing our children, students, players, and employees inward, teaching them that their thinking and feelings are naturally in flux. From a high feeling state, options are fruitful and empowering. But from a low feeling state, options are desperate and destructive.

Let's return to camp. Rather than disciplining when a camper's actions don't fit the counselors' definition of appropriate, here's an idea: Teach those fifteen-year-old boy campers, who are wavering between whether or not to raid the girls' cabin, that the "off" feeling in their stomachs is a sign that their thinking is momentarily off course. It's telling them that acting from this type of psychological disposition is not a good idea for anyone.

This might sound ambitious, but the path of no resistance toward growth and development is through an *understanding* of how the mind functions and the *nurturing* of free will, not through expectations, rules, and goals (more on goals next). After all, isn't childhood supposed to be a time when kids grow, discover, make mistakes, and prosper? Isn't it a time when free will is supposed to bloom?

WHERE GOALS TRULY ORIGINATE

Let's talk about goals. Goal setting is so commonly suggested that most people just assume it's the correct thing to do. Well, to me, chasing goals is incorrect. Goal setting is outside-in and circumstance driven. People never go through the process of setting goals from a high level of consciousness. Setting goals takes thought—a lot of thought.

Don't get me wrong. As conveyed in the last chapter, I love immersing myself in projects. But my projects have a better chance of making an impact on others, or succeeding, if I'm guided by imagination and instincts. Not by the narrow-minded pursuit of a goal (a thought) that randomly appears in my head.

Here's a demonstration that I often use in my talks: I look out into the audience and announce the goal of shaking hands with the person sitting in the middle of the last row. I then state the obvious: Chances are that I'll reach that goal in pretty short order. I'll narrow my focus and set my sights directly on that person—I won't be denied. The trouble, however, is that with my perceptual field narrowed, I block out all the people to my left and right. I can't see them as I make my way to my goal. And that means I'm missing something—the untapped opportunity in the experience of meeting each of these people.

To avoid missing opportunities, then, why not look to where goals truly originate? Your built-in capacity for inspiration and connection. That's what creative people do. Their minds rarely get jammed because they know that fixating on a goal—a stale thought about what they want to do today, this year, or in their lifetime—prevents evolution and growth. It limits the possibilities of the journey and binds them to yesterday.

My message on goals is simple: If you understand that thought is designed to fluently flow in and out, it won't make sense to hold thought in place by treating your goals as gospel. Insightful planning or decision making doesn't come from intellectually setting goals. It just comes.

―――――――

As an example of my message on goals, consider the struggles of the New York Jets football team since 2009, the year Rex Ryan became head coach. From the start, Ryan's mantra was the goal of winning the Super Bowl. On many occasions, he proclaimed, "My team is good enough to win it all; why be afraid to say it?" Well, there's nothing wrong about standing up for what you believe in. And if it feels right to say it, go ahead. Ryan's mistakes, I think, were buying into his arbitrary thoughts about the Super Bowl (not staying in the game) and stringently setting the goal in the first place.

Why were these mistakes? Because single-mindedness limited the creative potential of Ryan and his players. When people narrowly set their sights on a goal, they restrict their ability to imagine and adjust. So in setting his sights solely

on the championship, Ryan helped reduce the consciousness of his team. He did exactly what I warned of earlier: He
made the journey about achieving one objective, not about
the experience or unlimited promise along the way.

One final note on the true source of goals: I'm not saying
that a Super Bowl championship, or any aspiration, doesn't
have value. I'm saying there isn't value in detaching yourself
from other imaginative opportunities in the pursuit of it. In
2009, the New Orleans Saints relished the quest of captur-
ing the Super Bowl's Vince Lombardi Trophy, which they
won. But this triumph wasn't all about football. Rebuilding
the hopes of the people of their city after Hurricane Katrina
was the driving force behind the Saints' victory.

STAYING IN THE GAME OR CARROTS AND STICKS?

Just as mindlessly chasing goals is restrictive, so is adding
punishment (sticks) for a lack of achievement, or prizes
(carrots) for achievement. Success, as we've seen, cannot be
instilled from the outside. Retribution or accolades do not
incentivize people in the long run. They direct people away
from inner motivation and virtues.

In fact, over the years, the work of several leading experts
on motivation and behavior has demonstrated this very
argument. We're just beginning to learn about their inside-
out approach.

Earlier, I said there was an author who makes a lot of sense about productivity in the workplace. His name is Daniel H. Pink, and much of Pink's work is centered on introducing us to theories otherwise concealed. In his book *Drive: The Surprising Truth About What Motivates Us*, Pink sets out to show (among many topics) that goals, carrots, and sticks aren't what they're cracked up to be. He talks about the studies of sociologist Richard Titmuss and psychology professors Harry Harlow and Edward Deci. In one study, the conclusion (and this conclusion is prevalent in *Drive*) was that an external incentive did not lead to more of a desired behavior; it actually led to less. Reason being, "It tainted an altruistic act and 'crowded out' the intrinsic desire to do something good."[14]

This study, to be clear, did utilize data (as do others in *Drive*). But Pink presents such studies and findings in a "go figure out what they imply for you" kind of way. That's why I'm a fan of his work.

I even remember a time from my own teenage years that illustrates what Pink described about the failings of external incentives. Back when I played high school hockey, my dad tried to motivate me to lift weights. He reasoned that to score more goals, and up the odds that a college coach would recruit me, I needed to get stronger. He offered incentives to get me into the gym, and he threatened to revoke some of

---

14. Daniel H. Pink, *Drive: The Surprising Truth About What Motivates Us* (New York: Riverhead Books, 2009), 48.

my car privileges (sticks to a teenager, for sure) if I didn't. But much to his dismay, I didn't see it that way. I somehow knew that my ability to score goals in high school had little to do with building more muscle. So, in sync with *Drive*'s studies and deductions, I lied to him. Clearly not the behavior my father was looking for. Funny thing, though, when I joined my college hockey team, I realized—without prodding—that getting stronger was a key to success, so into the weight room I went.

———

Here at the end of chapter 4, let me restate: As my father and I learned, the path of no resistance can only be uncovered when you act from your own inner wisdom and allow realizations to find you. Besides, just as setting external goals doesn't motivate, achieving external goals or obtaining possessions isn't the link to fulfillment. Being a human being is the link. And staying in the game is what human beings are born to do.

At the hub of so many self-created problems and so much suffering today are people who don't stay in the game: They take meditative time-outs in order to fix temporary viruses of thought. Why does this cause suffering? Because taking time-outs, like all techniques, only corrupts the natural functioning of the system. It's a shortcut to well-being, similar to drinking alcohol to ease your pain. Take enough shortcuts and your life eventually unravels. Looking outside for well-being could take its toll on your family, friends, and coworkers, too.

By contrast, do you know someone who rarely seems to sweat the small stuff? Someone who lights up a room when he or she walks in? Someone who consistently makes a positive difference in his or her community? Someone who has no time for pettiness or judgment? Maybe this person even stands up to injustice, but resolutely remains composed.

That's the person who lives the message of this chapter, and that person *does* sometimes think insecure or aberrant thoughts. Everyone does.

The path of no resistance, however, is populated with people who succeed no matter what they are thinking. They know better than to look for quick fixes. Trying to find the zone only takes them further away. Rather than look outside to explain or manage their feelings, they stay in the game and effortlessly self-correct to clarity and understanding. And, most important, to love.

What happens when people self-correct to love? The answer might seem even more touchy-feely than our earlier discussion about feelings. It's just as essential, though. That's why I devote chapter 5 to love and other surprising sources of strength.

5.

THE UNIVERSAL RULE

*Everyone, it seems, has a different definition of the word "God"
these days, including spiritual teachers and religions. Most of
these definitions are complex, unbending, and wordy. I once
attended a service where a spiritual leader claimed: "It's up to
the individual to decide whether or not the word 'God' points
to some conceptual or intangible reality or not."*

*Say what? See what happens when we use our intellect to
explain truth?*

*When Sydney Banks was asked his definition of God, his
answer was simple and eloquent.*

His answer was "Love."

In the first four chapters of this book, we explored the true
source of the human experience. How, from the inside-
out, every person conjures up his or her reality. And since
the process only works one way, we talked about the risks
involved when someone does something on the outside in
order to improve his or her feelings on the inside.

That's why, as we discussed in chapter 4, the setting of rules, expectations, and goals—though they appear to work sometimes—can't generate long-term success. They are direction from the outside. But that's also why preventing yourself from setting rules, expectations, and goals isn't the complete answer either.

First and foremost, success (like all productive outcomes) is the result of clarity of thought or consciousness. From a high level of consciousness, we all pretty much fly by the seat of our pants, instinctively and free, acting without deliberate thought. Sure, we might plan (or envision how we're going to get from point A to point B) from this psychological perspective. But again, this type of planning isn't guesswork—it's insight. And insights come from you.

Rules are definitely a hard issue to get a handle on—and to let go of. In my experience, even people who value this inside-out perspective regarding rules will often ask, "Don't we need rules for households, teams, or companies to run efficiently? What about religions? They have codes of conduct and commandments that we're supposed to follow, don't they?" Perhaps. But to me, there's only one rule that is foolproof, and it's relevant to every organization or religion you can think of:

That rule is *love*.

Love is resilient, secure, and instinctual. Love looks beyond someone's behavior and toward understanding.

From love, excellence is effortless and leadership automatic. Love is the opposite of boxed in or uptight. Love is free.

Yet people seldom associate love with excellence, leadership, or success. Most of us, as you know, are too busy looking outside for their source. A pro hockey player once told me that he loved scoring goals. I said he had it reversed: Love comes first; goals will follow.

So starting now, let's resolve to look inward. To wisdom. To spirit. To truth. Perhaps you've already done so, at times, as you've read this book. If yes, then you understand what it's like to know (and see) that you feel your thinking and nothing on the outside: Everything turns wonderful; everything turns full of opportunity. I realize this may sound trite, or perhaps far-out, but I can only call the game as I see it. The first four chapters of this book have led us to the ultimate gift of looking within for answers; to the one thing in life that does not come from our ability to think; to the only thing that's real.

They've led us to love.

Onward and upward, let's now see what love can do.

THE SHIFT

Keep this inside-out suggestion in mind as we go further: No matter your behavior—including the setting of rules, expectations, and goals—if your actions come from love, then act, speak, and listen. If they do not come from love, then don't. Is that simple enough?

If not, here's more detail by way of a story. In September 2012, I agreed to caddie for one of my best friends, Jay Blumenfeld. Jay was attempting to qualify for the US Senior Amateur Golf Championship, the most prestigious amateur golf tournament in the world for players fifty-five and older. While Jay is an accomplished player, we both figured that having me "on the bag" might do him some good. And by a fluke, the qualifying round happened to be at my former home course in New Jersey.

This story, however, is not about our friendship, my assistance as a caddie, or Jay's qualifying round. This story is about what can happen when a person wakes up to the thought-feeling connection. It took place in the heat of the battle that day, as Jay and I walked off the fifteenth tee.

But first, let me tell you about the prior fourteen holes.

Jay was paired with a man named Val. Right off, it was obvious that Val was over his head in this tournament. He didn't have the skill (his game was subpar at best) or the golf etiquette to participate. Although not intentional, he often moved and talked when Jay was preparing to play his shots. He was a nice man, but for Jay, being paired with Val was about the worst break a player could get. In fact, over the first fourteen holes, my main responsibility was keeping Jay distracted from Val's antics—his thoughts about Val's antics,

I should say. A few times, though, I could sense my friend's blood about to boil.

Now, Jay understands inside-out, and he's a big proponent of my work. But even though I reminded him that Val was just another circumstance and, like all circumstances, was neutral, Jay felt so frustrated that there was no convincing him. Plus, this wasn't my first time around this block. I knew that Jay was either going to wake up to the thought-feeling connection (and recognize that his feelings were coming from inside of him) or he wasn't. There wasn't much I could do about it.

Meanwhile, Jay stood at even par through fourteen holes. It was a good score for most golfers, but not good enough on a course that I, his caddie, knew like the back of my hand. And not good enough to qualify for a tournament like this.

Then we climbed onto the fifteenth tee, facing a difficult hole with water up the entire right side of the fairway. Wouldn't you know it, as Jay took his club back for his tee shot, Val stepped right behind him. Jay pulled his ball left into the thick rough. This meant that on his next shot Jay's ball would have to carry over the water out of an awful lie. Things looked bleak, or so I thought, and as we walked off the tee I was ready for Jay to erupt in complaints. I was also prepared to advise him to stay in the game since he still had a chance to qualify with four holes left to play. But, amazingly, Jay spoke a different tune. He'd had an insight.

Jay said to me, "You know, maybe Val is getting over some kind of illness or something and that's why he can't play so well and his awareness isn't so good. Who am I to judge him? He's actually a good guy, and I've been treating him with disrespect all day."

Disrespect was a strong word, and I really didn't think Jay had acted that way. But the roller coaster was on its way up, so the last thing I was going to do was interfere. Rather, I said, "Right on. Now you're seeing it, buddy. Why don't you walk with Val down the fairway? I'll find your ball, no worries."

Here's where things got really interesting. I located Jay's ball in the deep rough, and to my delight, his lie wasn't so bad after all. Jay then arrived and, with an obvious shift in consciousness, told me what a lovely conversation he'd had with Val. He then pulled a club from his golf bag, swung, and sent his ball over the water and toward the green. It stopped five feet from the cup. He made the putt for a birdie, 3. He then parred the sixteenth hole, birdied the seventeenth, and birdied the eighteenth to close at 3 under par, qualifying for the US Senior Amateur Championship. Simply astonishing. What a performance!

———————

Obviously, Jay is one heck of a golfer. Three under par is a great score. For our purposes in this book, though, it's not his score that's significant—it's his journey down the path of no resistance. Even though frustrating thoughts kept coming, Jay's innate functioning and clarity eventually won out over any passing belief in his own shoddy thinking. Truth be told, this heightened level of consciousness was available throughout the first fourteen holes. It just took a momentary glimpse of love and compassion—an insight—for it to come flooding through.

What's more, do you recall when I said earlier that knowing and seeing that we feel our thinking creates opportunity? Then check this out: On three of the last four holes, Val's ball came to rest on the same line on the green as Jay's but farther from the cup. This meant that as Val putted on these crucial holes, Jay and I got a chance to watch the break (how the ball would roll) on Jay's upcoming putts. What luck. Thankfully, we were conscious enough to notice. Thankfully, Jay found the perfect playing partner in Val.

THE HIDDEN POWER OF OPENNESS AND UNDERSTANDING

As explained in chapter 3, wisdom unfolds from the inside (i.e., inner wisdom); it doesn't enter because of something a person does on the outside. But there's something else you should know: Love, compassion, understanding, respect, and openness form the foundation of your inner wisdom. They unfold from the inside, too.

Wonderful sentiments found Jay because he stayed in the

game, looked away from circumstance, and thus allowed his psychological immune system to do its thing (self-correct). The insight he experienced and the love he felt weren't imparted by Val, me, or even himself. Understanding how the system works—what Jay's judgmental feelings were saying to him—is what ultimately caused his consciousness to rise.

This relates back to our previous conversation about how it is self-defeating to *practice* (or try to achieve) awareness, mindfulness, or happiness. Ditto for love. You don't have to work on it. Realize it only flows in one direction, in to out, and love goes to work on you.

Never was this direction more evident to me than one April morning when, with school closed for break, my son Jackson and I hit the high school gym for a workout. The county baseball tournament was ahead, and Jackson wanted to get in some extra hitting and throwing practice.

Both of us felt light and free that morning. Vigorously, we attacked the workout. So much so that Jackson got on an awesome roll in the batting cage, smacking each ball I threw with effortless power.

But then, in a split second, everything changed.

The door to the gym slowly opened and in walked a young boy. The boy sat alone by the door and didn't say a word. All he did was stare at Jackson. With every swing my son took, the boy became more interested. Even standing up to take a few imaginary swings of his own. Jackson, however, didn't appreciate the sudden attention. He lost his groove. The effortlessness in the batting cage had become drudgery. It got so bad that my son (usually a model of inside-out) walked over to me and said, "This kid messed me all up. What's he doing here anyway?"

Yikes. I encouraged Jackson to keep swinging, but he wanted no part of it. Instead, he dropped his bat, ripped off his batting gloves, and stormed for the exit.

But then, in a split second, everything changed again.

Jackson took a detour on his way out. He walked over to the boy, offered him a spare glove, and invited him to play catch. The boy said his name was Ben, and his father was a custodian at the school. Ben eagerly accepted Jackson's overture. Together they played for about half an hour, with Jackson providing some basic instruction along the way. When they said their good-byes, Jackson gave Ben a spare cap, and Ben offered well wishes in the county tournament. On the way home, I said to my son, "What you just did was better than watching you hit a home run—and much more important to your future, and Ben's as well."

That was true, but deep down I also knew that Jackson was going to thrive in the county tournament. And he did.

———

The lesson in this example is threefold. First, understanding that our sensory experiences come from thought, and not circumstance, allows a person to behave judiciously and sensitively—even when he or she doesn't feel like it. In spite of his initial outside-in comment, Jackson knew that his own thinking, and not Ben's presence, had altered his momentum in the batting cage. Jackson's disgruntled feelings were not telling him to spurn Ben. His feelings were telling him: "You're not seeing things right. Now, go talk to the boy because if you were seeing things right—that's what you'd do!"

Second, being open to and understanding of others makes a person more competitive, not less. An open person is a conscious person. Again, when conscious, a person's perceptual field expands, allowing the person to sense the possibilities in all people and situations. This is a key to competitiveness *and* benevolence. Others might have ignored Ben or shooed him off. But Jackson became aware of Ben's interest in what he was doing and was open enough to explore where greeting him might lead. The same could be said of Ben's demeanor toward Jackson, by the way.

Last but not least, there's one lesson here that we don't want to miss. Let's hope that when Ben is in high school, he looks back and offers a young person the same openness and understanding that was shown to him. I bet he will. Acts like this are contagious, since they point us inward to our free will and inherent goodness. Almost always, they create a chain of love.

HOW MUCH DO YOU CARE?

Jackson and Ben's encounter confirms what we've learned so far: We can't control our level of consciousness or the thoughts that pop into our heads, but we can always prevent ourselves from behaving from self-centered states of mind.

Not acting on egotistical thoughts, in fact, snaps us back into clarity. As Jackson's father, I'm proud of the effort he puts into his baseball career and other aspects of his young life. I'm positive, however, that acts of generosity and compassion will have a larger impact on his level of long-term achievement. This applies to you and me, too.

So let's keep at it. Few people recognize the natural bond between love and enduring excellence. I don't want you to make the same mistake.

Have you ever noticed that you have to look far and wide to find a prejudiced or malicious preschool child? It's true. Simply observe two of them playing alone, and our built-in propensity to care for, and love, our fellow man becomes obvious. Absent of parental hovering, control, or judgment, it's virtually impossible for one child to put the needs of himself or herself above the other.

And guess what? If it weren't for learned behavior, your own care for others—acquaintances and total strangers—would flourish in the exact same fashion. Caring for others is part of human nature. No one is born selfish.

That's why I frequently use young children as illustrations

in this book. Their process of thought is pure and uncomplicated, so they don't spend a lot of time tending to the thoughts (even judgmental thoughts) that randomly pop into their heads. But as we age, we start paying attention to these random thoughts; our intellect ramps up, and our consideration for others becomes blurry. This happens, more or less, to everyone.

I speak from experience. In September 2012 (right before my caddie adventure), I was in the UK presenting for my buddy and colleague Jamie Smart, the author of *Clarity*. While there, I met a man who was having trouble locating a copy of *Stillpower*. As he described his frustration, my mind was immediately flooded with a solution, an insight: "When I get home, I'm going to send him a copy of the book straightaway." But then, for no discernible rhyme or reason, my thinking ramped up and spun me off course. I thought: "If I do that for him, I'll have to do it for each person at the event. My publisher won't like it. Perhaps, as an author, I'm not supposed to be so approachable, etc."

Lucky for me, however, I usually practice what I preach. At that moment, my personal thinking created a conceited and awful feeling in my gut, which was my sign to follow my instinctual sentiment of sending him a book. Which I did as soon as I returned home.

There's something else I want to share about our built-in propensity to care for others and how, unknowingly, it can get confusing. I once read a quote from Oprah Winfrey in which she said that being kind is the key to a contented and clear mind-set. This, to me, is not true. I love Oprah, and she's inspired the wisdom within many people, but she's got this one flipped.

This misunderstanding is common. Just go on Facebook or Twitter and you'll see tons of posts about the necessity of being compassionate, giving, or respectful. In *The Path of No Resistance,* however, we've learned that trying to act a certain way doesn't work. Being kind is not the key to a contented and clear mind-set. A contented and clear mind-set (inside) is the key to everything productive, including kindness and care for others (outside).

That's the reason this chapter on love falls where it does in this book. What preceded were explanations and demonstrations of how the system works. This chapter is about the wonderful repercussions of grasping the workings of the system. Those who don't grasp it often try to impart kindness and love from the outside.

But it won't work. You can't force yourself to care. You can't force yourself to love. The key is understanding why at times you don't feel loving and caring: It's the regular ups and downs of your thinking (a clear mind loves, a cluttered mind does not). Your life, including those around you, is never to blame.

Now, if only our relationships, marriages, or partnerships were that simple.

Well, they just might be.

THE NO-RESISTANCE PATH TO A HEALTHY PARTNERSHIP

Lisa and Bill grew up together, became high school sweethearts, went their separate ways in college, reunited afterward, and got married two years later. They have three children, exciting careers, and a lovely home in the suburbs. But they also had a list of day-to-day problems that they believed were causing an increasing level of marital strife.

Bill's company is a client of mine. So when Bill told me about the trouble at home, I suggested that he and Lisa come see me. Even though they had previously visited a marriage counselor to no avail, and even though counseling couples isn't my norm, I knew a paradigm existed that they had not explored. Bill agreed, and eight days later, he and Lisa arrived at my office, poised to hash out and get to the bottom of their list of problems.

"But not so fast," I told them. I had two requirements during our time together: "One, we don't try to fix your problems. Two, I will meet with both of you, but separately." While these requirements surprised both Lisa and Bill, they were determined to save their marriage, and nothing else was working, so we began.

Lisa was up first. After we settled in, I relayed something discussed repeatedly in this book: For all people, problems are the byproduct of their thinking and mind-set. From a level head, the same problematic circumstance is no longer so. As such, Lisa's alleged problems (one was Bill going fishing on Sunday mornings) weren't the reason for her current mood; they were the result of her current mood. Or, what Lisa experienced—Bill leaving early on Sunday mornings—didn't create her bound-up thinking. Bound-up thinking is why Bill leaving early on Sunday mornings bothered Lisa.

In fact, after some reflection, Lisa admitted, "Actually, sometimes I understand Bill's desire for peace and quiet, so I encourage him to go fishing. I don't mind it at all."

Now we were getting somewhere. I could see, as a new line of thinking took hold, the tension lifting from Lisa's shoulders. She then asked, "So, if I understand Bill and his actions better from a higher state of mind, what can I do to get there more often?"

I replied, "There's nothing you have to do. Just keep looking toward your own level of clarity and away from Bill's behavior. From a clear state of mind, you won't feel irritated by what Bill does; differences will easily be forgotten and problems easily solved. But from a cluttered state of mind, anything he does will irritate you."

I continued, "Knowing how you and all people, including Bill, form your personal reality [how the mind works] is all that's required of either of you."

But suddenly, Lisa's attitude seemed to change. She shook her head and forcefully asked, "Then why have we been trying to negotiate a fishing schedule, and other issues, that have nothing to do with how each of us feel to begin with?"

I couldn't answer *that* question. But nevertheless, it was an impressive insight. I simply said, "It's common in any type of mediation setting to focus on a problem, such as Bill's fishing, as if it's the cause of strife. But, again, problems aren't the cause of strife; they're a symptom of strife."

As we went on, Lisa felt more and more relaxed, and the insights kept coming. To her it was now clear: She and Bill were victims of an outside-in mix-up. Because they didn't know that feelings can only come from within, they had taken each other's behavior as the source of their feelings.

I then concluded by talking to Lisa about the simplicity in riding out any dubious feelings (staying in the game) until fresh thinking arrives and answers become obvious— whatever those answers may be. And just between you and me: I didn't say this to Lisa (and it wasn't the case for her and Bill), but sometimes the insightful answer is for partners to go their separate ways.

Before she departed, Lisa hugged me and then exclaimed, "I can't wait for Bill to learn this, too!"

Thankfully, my time with Bill played out much like it did with Lisa. As he left my office and headed to the room where she was waiting, I noticed that he also seemed more at ease. The next thing I knew, Lisa and Bill walked out of my office—arm in arm.

THE MISDIRECTION OF HATE

The reason that divorce is so prevalent today is hiding in plain sight. It's the same reason for so much violence in our communities, and the same reason that we live in a world of haves and have-nots. We just don't know that we're wired to feel nothing but our own thinking. We're convinced that we feel things made of matter, like money. Or that someone's actions can make us feel a certain way. Or that our ethnicity, job title, or where we live can define us. This distortion could drive anyone—including you and me—to hateful or irrational behavior toward another person.

This is not to say that opposing others is wrong. I happen to love competition or going head-to-head with someone else. But what I've grown to understand is that competition, at its root, is a form of *cooperation* in disguise. Competing authors in this book's category, for example, are actually pushing me, supporting my quest to raise my game and get better. These authors are a necessary component of my career. Hating them is the last thing that's going to work to my benefit. I might disagree with other authors, and as you can see I'm not shy about saying it, but if the disagreement gets personal, I've lost my way.

Moreover, it's not that I always feel cooperative with my competitors; that's unfeasible. But what I just said feels right to me. Hating or disrespecting another person feels wrong. I choose the path of no resistance. I choose the path that feels right. At least, the majority of the time I do. That's the path I hope you will choose as well.

Still, it's important to restate that everyone is capable of having hateful or disrespectful thoughts about anything—including about someone else. You're not psychologically deranged if you think that you want to wring someone's neck. Hateful actions, however, are a different can of worms. There's never, ever, a gun to your head forcing you to act on your thoughts, whatever those thoughts might be.

To not act from hate, though, a person *must* understand where hate originates.

Consider a person who has just been fired from a job. Odds are that this person's thoughts about his or her former boss won't exactly be kind. They might even be downright hateful. But while it appears that these thoughts are the result of the boss's actions (firing this person), they're actually the culmination and continuation of a capricious pattern of thinking. A short time before the person was fired, one negative thought led to another, and then to another. Pretty soon his or her mind-set and level of consciousness were in the dumps. The result: dismal performance on the job and, ultimately, termination.

Hate, if you look closely at it, can only come from inside of us. It's actually another misinterpretation of one's feelings (like Lisa and Bill's marital strife). In this instance, being fired is not the cause of the person's insecure and hateful thoughts. Being fired is a symptom of believing and focusing on such thoughts, which built up, affected performance, and led to the firing. This is an essential distinction to make. Why? Because when people try to hunt down the source of their insecurity, errant thoughts accumulate, state of mind lowers, and the chance for bad behavior goes up.

It's a fait accompli: People who don't understand the true (inner) source of their feelings will almost always search outside. That's when their behavioral goose becomes cooked, and actions can turn vicious. Just watch the news on TV. You'll find story after story of men and women looking outside for answers and, as a result, taking their anguish and rage out on what they find: possibly a former boss or anyone with a difference of opinion.

Test this for yourself. During volatile moments in your own life, were your emotions and behavior the result of the circumstance or person you encountered, or your mindset when you encountered the circumstance or person? Understanding that feelings can only come from inside of you cuts rage and hateful behavior off at the pass.

THE ONENESS OF SUCCESS

It's no secret. This book is about pointing you inward, to how the minds of human beings work, what we all have in common, and why we feel what we feel. Think again about Maria Venegas's mood chart. It's little wonder that hate was the lowest feeling on the scale. But Maria didn't say it was wrong for her students to feel that way. She merely showed them that it wasn't wise to look outward when they did. The mitigation of hate rests within.

Love, respect, and togetherness are much simpler sentiments than hate. Love requires no thought. We experience love, and express it, without effort. Have you ever watched a person rejoice in victory and felt good inside? Have you ever witnessed someone overcome apparently enormous obstacles and become inspired? Have you ever felt sad about another person's loss? What you're experiencing is a divine phenomenon called the "oneness of life." It's important, I think, to now talk about why this phenomenon occurs and what can be learned from it.

As we've discussed, the identical spiritual and formless energy runs through everyone. Meaning, you feel the experience of another because we're all fragments of the same spiritual puzzle. That's why the condition of the world (and our own lives) would improve by leaps and bounds if only we'd start stressing our similarities and stop talking about our perceived differences.

By a long shot, I'm not the only one who has spoken about the oneness of life and looking within for answers. Much wiser men and women than I have done their best to point us in this freeing direction: Abraham Lincoln, Mother Teresa, Jackie Robinson, Gloria Steinem, Robert Kennedy, Mahatma Gandhi, Martin Luther King Jr., John Lennon, and Sydney Banks, to name a few.

The big picture, however, continues to grow distorted. Since most of us miss that we each live in a separate (and ever-changing) reality governed by personal thought, our natural sense of harmony is slipping away.

But this trend is reversible. Why? Because everyone creates their separate reality in the exact same way—via thought. *That* is what we all have in common. Realize that the oneness of life is essential in your own quest for happiness and success, and the momentum shift just might start with you. Better yet, it *will* start with you. People automatically wither in an environment of isolation, ego, and contempt. People automatically thrive when they stop making circumstantial excuses for their feelings. They find clarity, take judgment off the table, and then feel a connection with everything around them.

This paradigm pertains to all aspects of life, even ultra-competitive settings like professional sports. This might surprise you, but Super Bowl winner Tyrone Keys once told me that during his pro football career he consistently felt love and respect for his opponents. And these feelings did not make Tyrone soft on the field. He was an extremely zealous and, at times, ferocious player. Respect and love fueled Tyrone's achievements, revealing a level of consciousness that freed him to be his best.

Likewise, on the PGA and LPGA golf tours, players are often found sharing their thoughts about the golf swing or a strategy for a particular course with their opponents. Now why do you suppose a golfer would help someone whom he or she is also trying to beat?

Go back to the notion of competition serving as a form of cooperation. Essentially, the oneness of life is this exact notion in action. Feel a common bond with others and your life is guaranteed to soar. Not only that, oneness can change the world. It can end prejudice, stop wars, and wipe out famine. Why is this so? Because, again, beyond the physical, the one thing you share with every person alive is the fact that you think. Circumstances vary, but the same struggles—born from thought—find us all.

The principle of thought, therefore, is the one place where answers to humanity's problems can be found. Thought, not circumstance, is why everyone gets bad feelings, why sometimes we hate. It's also why, in the face of matching circumstances, we love. Our thinking untangles, we open up from inside to out, and like magic, our perspective on the world and each other changes.

Remember this as we advance: Everyone is blessed, and cursed, with the spiritual quality of thought. It doesn't matter where you're from or what you believe in—*all human beings are connected.* You can close yourself off from certain people if you want. You can think you have something that others might lack. But if you do, you won't find happiness or enduring success because you're looking outward. The path of no resistance runs the opposite way.

Isn't it time we look inside and recognize our common

bond? We're in the soup together, people—there's no escaping it.

WHAT HURRICANE SANDY TAUGHT ME ABOUT THE PRINCIPLE OF THOUGHT

Here's an episode that most of us have in common and know all too well: traffic accidents. Have you ever noticed how unruffled people seem in the aftermath of traffic accidents? Cars collide and get damaged, days are thrown into tizzies, and sometimes people get hurt. But in the midst of all this, people are generally rational and cooperative. How come? Hold that question; we'll come back to it in a minute.

First, back to a not-so-common episode. In chapter 4, I talked about Hurricane Sandy. For a week, in October 2012, my family had no power or water at home, and our property took a beating from the storm. But we were lucky. Like most people up and down the East Coast of the United States, we were physically fine and psychologically resolute. Our community pulled together. In spite of the circumstances, compassion and determination showed us the way.

More than two years have now passed since the hurricane. In its wake, I often find myself reflecting on the relatively upbeat and supportive mood of the people of my region during that period—and what it can teach us. Specifically: Why can't we pull together like that all the time? Does it take a hurricane to reveal our innate ability to take swift and creative action, to reveal our natural concern for our fellow man?

Can you answer those questions? Hopefully, our dialogue about oneness helped. If you can, we've made some progress. You understand the principle of thought, which also means you've found the secret to happiness—and resilience.

This is how the answer seems to me: Thoughts and feelings of love and peace are divine and true. Bound-up and judgmental thoughts and feelings are false, a sham. So, when we don't have time to overthink things (like during a disaster), human beings instinctively care, and our behavior is almost always courteous and creative. When we have time to overthink, insecurity and ego creep in. We mistakenly believe this thinking to be meaningful, and our behavior often turns self-serving and hollow.

A few days after we got our power back after Hurricane Sandy, I almost fell into this trap. I bumped into a friend at a local diner. His family still had no power, heat, or water. He looked tired and cold. Because my family didn't need our portable generator anymore, I immediately had the wonderful feeling that I should offer it to my friend. In fact, this was the same feeling I described earlier in this chapter when I wanted to send the man in the UK a copy of *Stillpower*.

And, once again, this selfless sensation was followed by less-giving thoughts: "What if we lose power again? Then I'd have to worry about asking for the generator back. That would be so awkward. Maybe I shouldn't be so charitable."

Fortunately for my friend (and me), though, I didn't buy in to my self-centeredness. I knew that my initial unforced and loving feeling suggested the proper course of action, while the uptight feeling that accompanied my selfish thoughts suggested just the opposite.

This is what Hurricane Sandy taught me about the principle of thought: Charity and efficiency come from clarity and intuition. Arrogance and incompetence come from what I just mentioned: overthinking.

No, it's not Hurricane Sandy—a circumstance—that brought out the best in the people of my area. You and I both know better than that. What brought out our best is that we didn't have many spare moments (like I had in the diner) to think and get stuck in our own temporarily misguided heads. So our inner wisdom, instincts, and love provided a clear and steadfast direction *without resistance*. This direction, as you're finding out, is available at any time, under any condition.

Back to my original question about traffic accidents and those moments of resolute feelings and action afterward. Do you know the answer now?

OUR CHARGE

Our look at love and other surprising sources of strength— compassion, understanding, respect, openness, kindness, care, cooperation—is not meant to obscure the central theme of this book: The degree to which you see that you feel your thinking and not your circumstances is what determines your ability to contribute to, and not take from, the world in which you live.

So, at this juncture, let's take this central theme and blend it together with this chapter's message. (The blender's about to get loud, so be ready.)

From where I sit, there is no time to waste. We must take stock of the current plight of our world. There's no longer any excuse to keep relying on the same tried-and-untrue, outside-in performance concepts, coping mechanisms, and psychological analyses that have failed us for years.

In short, our collective level of clarity is waning today. Our hang-ups are on the rise, and we keep looking outside to explain why. If you're not excelling at work right now, I'm sorry, but the economy is not to blame. If your marriage resembles *The War of the Roses*, it's not your spouse's fault. And my biggest concern is not that we're attributing our feelings to our bosses, employees, friends, or significant others—it's that we're also holding our children responsible. Not on purpose, mind you. But when things don't appear quite right, we're forgetting that we each establish our reality from in to out. Our children and their behavior do not account for what happens inside of us.

Due to our own uncertainty, then, we're pigeonholing our kids with haphazard opinions and diagnoses. We're setting up treatment plans, and looking for newer and newer excuses—for our own feelings—as we go. How many more kids do we have to label with ADHD, for instance, before we realize that in many cases we're fabricating mental illness? We're not cherishing the innate mental health that rests within everyone. Our kids will be fine. We will be fine. Let's promote free will and instincts, not destroy them.

Adults, it's our charge. We need to get our acts together and stop perpetuating this outside-in cycle. We need to relearn how the system works and stay in the game. You can counsel your children; you can discipline. Yet nothing will work at those moments when you feel the slightest sense of resistance inside of you. Or insecurity. Or judgment.

And one more thing: You chatted on the telephone when you were in high school; that was your form of socializing. Your kids are on the Internet; that's how they connect. The Internet is outside—there's always a circumstance to blame. Look inside. The answers are there.

TEN INNOVATIVE IDEAS TO WAKE UP YOUR ORGANIZATION

It might not happen overnight; it might not happen this week; it might not happen this month. But looking inside toward thought means that it will happen. You're going to self-correct to clarity—to love—and then find impactful answers for you, your children, or any group to which you belong. It's foolproof. The more you turn away from what takes place on the outside in order to justify what you feel on the inside, the simpler and more splendid life becomes.

For now, though, let's take a breath and pause for a brief review. Since we're all after waking up to clarity and consistency, reflect on the following innovative ideas and see if any of them make sense for your family, team, school, or organization. These ideas highlight some of our progress so far, and they'll help moving forward. Remember: Pay attention to the insights that spring from these ideas, not to the ideas word for word.

1. *Keep goal setting to a bare minimum, if instituted at all.*

   Goal setting narrows focus, limits opportunities, and shrinks the perceptual field. Wanting to win is great, but instead of single-mindedly setting your sights on winning, relish the journey and experience. If you do, the imaginative path to happiness and success will become evident on its own.

2. *Recognize and embrace individuality.*

   Even within team environments, it's essential that individuality be fostered and encouraged. Why? Free will is an essential ingredient to productive behavior. People will simply not perform to the best of their ability if their intuition or personal thought systems are compromised.

3. *Limit rules and expectations.*

   Codes of conduct are very slippery slopes. The conflict between what a person thinks is right and what an organization tells the person is right will, more often than not, bind and confuse the person. This inner bewilderment creates dysfunction—and failure.

4. *Encourage love for, and respect of, opponents.*

   Love and respect are the ultimate symptoms of consciousness. Hate and disrespect come from a lack of consciousness. So just ask yourself, "How do I feel when I'm not considerate of others, when I resent my competition, or when I hold them in contempt?" Now, why would you ever want your organization to perform from this insecure psychological perspective?

5. *Discourage the creation of a pecking order.*

   When people operate from low levels of clarity, they dwell on their differences. They become insulated and egotistical, and in a team setting, certain members often appear more valuable than others. Not so. Although roles and talents vary, if you remove one piece of the pie, your organization ceases to be whole and its natural chemistry and functioning become limited.

6. *Do not stress communication.*

Here's something to look forward to in chapter 6. An often-missed reason that organizations fail is because people overcommunicate—they speak and listen when they're not able to do so productively (they're in a low mind-set). Lack of communication is never a real issue. A person's state of mind when he or she communicates, or doesn't, is the key to rapport between teammates, coworkers, or family members.

7. *Do not endorse a "culture."*

When an organization endorses once-successful traditions or ethics, it's adopting someone else's recollection of the way to perform, which is not pertinent now. Buying into a culture is massively outside-in. It thwarts free will and creates followers who aren't capable of coming through in the big moment.

8. *Leave the past in the past.*

The past, like a culture, is simply a thought system carried through time. No matter how hard you try, you can't replicate a former triumph, technique, or feel. They're smoke; they no longer exist. Besides, current team members could care less about the good old days. When their heads are clear, they intuitively live in the present—don't lead them away from it.

9. *Drive effort with freedom.*

Most organizations continue to revere and promote a grind-it-out paradigm that has little to do with success. Achievement is the result of clarity, passion, and freedom—not diligence, desperation, or hard work. When people don't give their best, there's one underlying reason: They're trying to control a natural instinct—effort. A self-defeating mistake.

10. *Find answers in state of mind, not behavior.*

All behaviors spawn from a person's state of mind. That's why this idea is the foundation of this list. We'll cover leadership soon, but for now: Looking to the state of mind of the members of your organization, and not to their behavior (punctuality, attitude, output), is the best example you can set.

THE RELEVANCE OF LOVE

Picture this: Yours truly, standing in front of a professional hockey or football team and suggesting that love is the key to great performance. And, as the players look at me like I'm some kind of fruitcake, I declare that this particularly applies to loving their opponents. For sure, some of the gazes and responses I've gotten over the years have been skeptical. But no matter, I'm certain it's true. Plus, talking about love wakes the players up to the fact that they're about to hear something different. I've got their attention, so off we go.

Even subscribers to my newsletter sometimes comment that they'd rather read about performance, or resilience, than love and our other surprising sources of strength. Touchy-feely sentiments, they might say, aren't usually associated with success. They don't know me very well. I'm not after usual. I'm after truth.

That's why, before we turn our attention to chapter 6, I want to make sure that no stone's left unturned. So just in case love remains superfluous to you, consider what follows. Let's call it the CliffsNotes version of chapter 5.

If you want to consistently perform at your best, love is especially relevant because it doesn't require deliberate thought. It's the byproduct of consciousness. When a person uncovers a high level of consciousness, insights flow and answers—including how to stay ahead of the competition—become obvious. By contrast, when a person exists at a low level of consciousness, the intellect gets overworked and answers slip away.

The purpose of this chapter about love, then, is simple: to turn you inward toward your most potent psychological disposition, and not outward toward willpower, disrespect, or following someone else's thought-based system or techniques. All of which divorce you from intuition. As I inferred about performers at their finest moments: They don't think—they're free. They don't work—they feel. To them, everything is seen as an asset or opportunity.

Now *that* sounds like love to me.

But what if you're not at your best and not immersed in love? There's no grounds for alarm. Look inside. Struggles only persist when we search outside for causes and cures. The path that we're on in this book points away from anything that saps our instincts by adding thought to our pursuit of excellence.

———————

To be candid, this chapter was by far the most intricate one to write. Talking this extensively about love (and hate, too) was a deviation, of sorts, from my standard operating procedure. But it was necessary. At the end of the day, knowing why we seem to fall in and out of love with life, or with our partners, or even with our children is the ultimate liberation. We feel our own thinking—not things, events, or people. This wisdom removes any chance of making molehills into mountains. It frees and makes life simple.

Syd Banks unwaveringly claimed, "The only thing that's real in life is love. Everything else is an illusion brought about by our thinking." Nothing could ring more true.

Also, I can't speak for you, but for me, understanding that it works the same for all of us clarifies the actions and suffering of others. It prevents me from judging. Don't forget:

We can only help someone when we're clear and lack judgment. The frailty of the human condition—that we think—explains everything.

In this chapter, I hope you've seen, too, that some of the standard beliefs about competition, relationships, caring, and parenting just might be missing the mark. Most important, though, perhaps love is a more far-reaching potion than we ever imagined. Love, it turns out, is universal.

So, where is this book taking you from here? We turn next to the simplicity of the path of no resistance—and what happens when we do and don't complicate it.

6.

A SIMPLE PATH

I once gave a talk to the students at Seton Hall University. Unbeknownst to me, a well-known (and totally outside-in) sports psychologist was in attendance. After the talk, I was surprised to find the psychologist in the group of people who wanted to say hello or ask me a private question or two. I saved him for last.

When we met, the psychologist said, "I'm intrigued by your perspective, but here's my question: If you're working for an NFL team whose kicker is about to attempt a field goal to win the Super Bowl, isn't it your job to get him in the right frame of mind to make the kick?"

My response: "No, my job is to help the kicker see that whether or not he makes the kick—his life will be perfectly okay."

On a cold and windy December day in Cleveland, Ohio, I arrived at the offices of the Cleveland Indians for a meeting with the team's president, Mark Shapiro. We talked about the inside-out paradigm that I teach. The approach was new to Mark, and it suggested many inventive possibilities for his team.

Yet, the last thing that Mark mentioned was the most memorable that day. He said, "Garret, what I respect about your work the most is how resolutely certain you are that the human mind works the way you describe."

I thanked him and then quickly replied, "I hope it doesn't come off as arrogant, but I just don't see one shred of possibility that external circumstances can actually affect the way people feel." I still don't.

To come full circle from what I said in the beginning, this book isn't about theories and concepts that are someone's personal opinion and open to interpretation or conjecture. This book is about principles, about truth. And principles and truth aren't open to interpretation or conjecture. They're universal and stand the test of time. Sure, we all doubt on occasion, but that's because we're each spiritual entities, making our way through this concrete world of form. It's this exact duality that confuses us and, if we think into that confusion, lowers our spirits and causes distress. Act from distress—well, you know what might occur.

This doesn't mean that the way I have presented this simple and at the same time revolutionary paradigm isn't open to disagreement. It certainly is. Here's my request on that front, though: Please take some time with any protests that feel personal or compulsive. Let them sit. As I've described, your feelings are your guide.

That said, here's an issue that critics do sometimes bring up: Every now and then they want proof of the value added when a person grasps the thought-feeling link. A critic might ask, "Where's the hard-and-fast evidence supporting the central theme of this book?" Okay, I'm game to answer. In a manner of speaking, that is.

Empirical evidence does not exist for the biological process of taking a breath. Everyone does it; we don't need proof. Similarly, we don't need proof or empirical evidence for the spiritual process of thinking. We all just do it.

I can't prove why we think, either. Nor will I try. And if that doesn't make sense to you, here's something else to mull over: You can't measure levels of consciousness or understanding. They're formless, just like the spiritual energy that runs through you and me. Attempting to find a formless entity through calculations, by compiling statistics, or under a microscope is foolhardy. Some scientists are trying hard to do it these days, particularly in the study of mindful meditation. But again, using science to explain truth, consciousness, or spirit is adding intellect to a formless understanding. It's not possible. Not to me anyway.

Let's return to William James, the father of modern psychology. He warned about this very direction and feared what might happen if we continued to use intellectual analysis to explain our psychological and behavioral shortcomings. Later, Martin Luther King Jr. also spoke out against this faulty direction. He cautioned, "Our scientific power has outrun our spiritual power. We have guided missiles and misguided men."[15]

Geez, was he on point.

You know the field-goal kicker that the sports psychologist asked me about earlier? The reason I won't provide an external method to help him find the "optimum" mind-set is because adding personal thought to a spiritual process, as William James and Dr. King revealed, is never advantageous. The kicker *will* be okay no matter what. As we've observed, that's the way the mind works: stale thinking out, fresh thinking in. Funny thing, though, the deeper the kicker sees it for himself, the better the odds become that he will make that winning kick. Marry the form and the formless and you have the path of no resistance in your back pocket.

SOMETHING TO BELIEVE IN

We've all experienced this to be true: Find some distance from your disconcerted thinking (and low feelings) and new horizons will suddenly appear. Life, as they say, has an interesting way of working itself out.

As I explained, two decades ago I was the epitome of wound-up and miserable. I was searching and striving for help. But with every outreach and method I followed, my

---

15. Martin Luther King Jr., *Strength to Love* (1977; Minneapolis: Fortress Press, 1981), 76.

reality grew bleaker. Then, thanks to a jarring insight, I leapt off my old misaligned path, stopped looking outside for answers, and crazy-good things started to happen.

One of which was author Richard Carlson (of *Don't Sweat the Small Stuff* fame) spending time on the phone with me, a complete stranger. Inspired by another of his books, *You Can Be Happy No Matter What*, and no longer desperate, I called Richard to discuss my jarring insight and to learn more about his unique beliefs. He pointed me inward to the source of this insight, introduced me to his mentors, and the rest took care of itself. (That's the short and unbelievable story of how the heck I got into this line of work.)

Here's another example, this time from my father's life, of what happens when a person finally stops compounding imaginary barriers, looks inward, and then finds happiness. My dad's been married three times and gone through two messy divorces. He's a cool guy, and I love him very much. But obviously marriage was not his forte. My dad didn't grasp inside-out. He believed that the perfect wife was a key to finding the secure feeling state that all people desire. We know by now how that type of quest turns out.

Then one day, my dad met Lynne. They've been married for more than twenty years.

Now, most of his friends think it's because of Lynne that my dad is a changed man. And she is special. But so were my mother and first stepmother. This guy married three of the prettiest, most generous, and most loving women on the planet. Trust me, I know my dad better than anyone. The reason for his newfound happiness: He's taken his foot off the gas pedal. He's found faith. *He's* the one who has changed—his wives are neutral.

And if by chance you're thinking that it might be age, or time, that's mellowed my dad, please reread chapter 2 and the beginning of chapter 4. Inside-out is all-encompassing.

There is, however, one uncanny aspect of old age that I would like to toss around: Generally, as people get up in years, they start to lose their attachment to the external world of form. They shrug and say, "Whatever," or "It is what is," when talking about day-to-day wants and frivolous needs that they once thought were important. Then when death rolls around, it gets real interesting. We've all heard stories about near-death experiences and people seeing light, feeling spirit, and touching heaven.

But guess what? Heaven is not a place. It's a level of consciousness available to you right now. Don't wait. Something to believe in doesn't exist on the outside, and that includes heaven.

As I see it in hindsight, my aim in this book has been to point you in an uncompromising direction—inward. But like my dad and many of the individuals I've used as examples, most of us look the opposite way. We search for something to believe in—out there. We look to the past or future; to a spouse, parent, or child; to our customs or morals; to our nationality; to wealth; even to a specific form of a higher power at times. What I hope you now realize is that we only do this when we're hurting or down on our luck. When consciousness elevates, "down on our luck" instantly morphs into "lucky."

In this very realization lies the possibility to rise above anything.

The Path of No Resistance was written to wipe away years of misinformation that's shrouded what you inherently know to be true: Feelings of struggle are never permanent. They're formless, not real, an illusion. They're the byproduct of the ever-changing nature of thought. Without a doubt, my own unshrouded understanding of this principle is what's changed my life. That's why, when I temporarily feel low today, it no longer occurs to me to manage my thinking or outlook. I stay in the game, and my thinking and outlook readily restore.

You, of course, are no different. When your level of confidence, satisfaction, or understanding for others declines, your pain does not come from the world around you. It comes from within you—from your thinking. So regardless of what occurs on the outside in a world of form, your perceptions of these events are formless and predetermined to change. Understand and believe in that principle, and your life will never be the same again.

OVERCOMING OBSTACLES

Did you notice that I just put "understand" before "believe in"? That's because I'm insisting that understanding how something works, rather than trying to do something (like telling yourself to believe) is the key to clarity, confidence, and excellence.

For example, many of my clients recognize that at times they overthink. But it's common for them to ask me, "What can I do to stop thinking?"

The answer is nothing. Understanding why they're overthinking—human beings are thinkers—is what slows down thought. Again, look outward to explain a noisy mind and your thinking gets louder. Look inward and it quiets.

Belief in yourself works the same way.

For this reason, I take umbrage with parents, coaches, teachers, and employers who tout belief or confidence as a performance booster. "Believe in yourself" is a common slogan, but it's empty rhetoric that takes people down a resistant path. You can't *try* to believe. Those who do often wonder why confidence can't be summoned at will. They're the ones who look outside to a surplus of artificial options (mental techniques, PEDs) to find confidence, which only magnifies their lack of it.

Instead, if you really want to find faith, or help another person find it, simply notice that belief and your current mind-set work in tandem. When your level of clarity is high, you believe; when it's low, you don't. Belief is that straightforward. Enduring answers always are.

Speaking of belief, or confidence, I hope that you're now considering the possibility that acting extrinsically (back to doing again) is not the key to improving it. Sure, most of today's popular motivational gurus disagree with me. They believe that intervention, or purposely changing one's thinking and/or circumstance, is the key to improving mental outlook. So, to dispel any lingering uncertainty, let's look at this misconception one last time.

Not long ago, one of these gurus, Tony Robbins, said in an interview that he helped raise the consciousness of a housebound young man who was paralyzed from the neck down by traveling with him to exotic destinations, sky-diving with him, and doing all sorts of exciting activities. Robbins claimed that in experiencing these external pursuits, this man silenced his negative thoughts and feelings, found inner resilience, and, ergo, lifted his mind-set.

Many people see Robbins as a savior, but talk about outside-in—and misguided effort. These activities might temporarily divert attention, but they're still neutral. State of mind is not linked to environment. No matter where the man goes, both his troubles and the answers to his troubles tag right along. Do all people who travel to beautiful places automatically become peaceful and rejuvenated? Of course not. I know for me, sometimes going on vacation seems to clear my head; while at other times, not so much.

That's why motivational specialists like Robbins believe (innocently but inaccurately) that a premeditated change of circumstance, environment, or thinking can elevate well-being and assist us in overcoming obstacles. Undeniably, there are times when a person does something, like take a vacation, skydive, or visualize success, and then finds himself or herself in a higher state of mind. But it's not because of "the doing" that belief or happiness is uncovered. It's because, no matter "the doing," the person has arbitrarily defaulted—self-corrected—to clarity and consciousness.

––––––––––

Earlier, I said that there are some current experts in productivity and motivation whose work I do admire, such as Daniel H. Pink. Another is a psychology instructor at Stanford University. Her name is Kelly McGonigal.

McGonigal wrote an out-of-the-ordinary book, *The Willpower Instinct*, which, when I first received a copy, I passed off as another blueprint for willing your way to success. But then I looked deeper. In the book, McGonigal presents a comprehensive counterargument to Robbins and other "outside-in'ers" who suggest doing something—such as taking control of, or intentionally distracting ourselves from, our pessimistic thoughts—as a way to rise above hardship. She instructs her audience to "feel what you feel, but don't believe everything you think." Sound familiar?

More fitting, she concludes:

Trying to control our thoughts and feelings has the opposite effect of what most people expect. And yet rather than catch on to this, most of us respond to our failures with more commitment to this misguided strategy. We try to push away thoughts and feelings we don't want, in a vain attempt to keep our minds safe from danger. If we want peace of mind and better self-control, we need to accept that it is impossible to control what comes into our minds. All we can do is choose what we believe and what we act on.[16]

We don't agree on everything, but clearly McGonigal, an award-winning psychologist, is blazing her own inside-out path. She intimates that obstacles are merely figments of our own thoughts. So if you try to control them, they will control you.

As for my take: Overcoming doesn't require one ounce of doing. You're built for it to just happen.

APPLICATION VERSUS UNDERSTANDING

There's a hidden gem of wisdom in the emotional football movie from the 1970s, *Brian's Song.* In the film, Chicago

---

16. Kelly McGonigal, *The Willpower Instinct: How Self-Control Works, Why It Matters, and What You Can Do to Get More of It* (New York: Avery, 2012), 234.

Bears teammates and roommates Gale Sayers and Brian Piccolo are competing for the starting running back position. Sayers, who turned out to be one of the best running backs in football history, is winning the job by a mile when Piccolo asks him, "Gale, do you *think* when you make all those great moves on the field or are you just running?"

Sayers answers, "Gee, Brian, I never considered it before, but I suppose I'm just running."

To which Piccolo shrewdly responds, "Well, can you start thinking? I want to play!"

To a certain extent, the following sequence pertains to us all: Like Sayers on the field, we're born with just the right amount of wisdom and instinct to navigate through any life situation. This wisdom and instinct, however, get trampled by the outside-in instruction of others. Then our insides churn with confusion. We overthink: "I know it's inside-out, but maybe it works outside-in, too. Is that even possible?"

Follow your feelings. The answer, once more, is no.

But don't mistake me. From our present level of consciousness, we're all doing what we think is right, which is the best we can do. Those in the self-help field are trying to help; most of them just don't get how the system works. If a person is cooped up in his or her apartment, depressed and lonely, rousing excursions are not the answer. Trying to instill belief or confidence is not the answer. This person is trapped in a misunderstanding. This person accepts most thoughts as real; to him or her, the world is flat.

As I've clarified throughout *The Path of No Resistance*, that's part of the explanation for many people's agony today. They seek advice, and the advice they get spins their heads even more. The one thing I suggest to every person with whom I work—including you right now—is to *not* take the inside-out paradigm introduced in this book and apply it strategically to an external issue. The realization that you feel your thinking isn't a strategy. You don't need a strategy—or a mechanic for your mind. When fortuitous insights start flooding through your system, then you're getting somewhere. The implications of these insights will open doors far beyond what you've ever deliberately considered.

Along these lines, I recently spoke to a college baseball pitcher who was struggling to throw strikes. To his initial amazement, our conversation was centered on how thought works and included almost nothing about what he thought was bothering him: his baseball career. But by the time we were done talking, he was clear, composed, and determined to unravel what, to him, were more big-picture-type issues. He wanted to help solve hunger in his community and support the victims of a gay-bashing incident on his college campus. What's more, in his next game, he struck out ten batters, only gave up four hits, and won 3–0. There are no limits; the possibilities are infinite.

I can't oversell it: Self-help methods requiring planned application run the risk of inhibiting your free will, instincts, and opportunities. They cry out: "Your way's not good enough; try this instead." A book that offers twelve steps to happiness will insist that these steps be studied, absorbed, practiced, and applied for them to work. And, as we discussed back in chapter 1, success experts who espouse positive thinking want you to watch out for both unconstructive and constructive thoughts, and then take time to replace the bad thinking with the good.

Man, this stuff is complicated.

And further, it doesn't make sense to call these methods "self-help" strategies. Strategies that must be thought about and applied are, in truth, external-help strategies. Answers for you are not found in anything or anyone external to you. They're found within you.

Is that now clear? I hope so. Because here's the coolest part of the inborn system we've reviewed in this book: Once you understand that the nature of your thinking is variable, it won't make sense (when you're struggling) to apply a strategy to change something that's not damaged and is designed to change on its own. Strategies require doing; doing requires thought; *thought is what creates struggle.* You wouldn't smoke cigarettes to cure the lung cancer they caused. We want less thought—not more!

This, on the other hand, is how it's supposed to work: Last fall I felt down; two of my three children had gone off to college. My head was filled with pessimistic thoughts: Where have the years gone? Am I getting old? What am I going to do? But then, without doing or changing anything,

I felt optimistic as insights and possibilities about my freed-up future flooded through me.

It happens to me; it happens to you: Bound-up feelings, at times, crop up. And because it looks like these feelings are caused by the world around us, applying a coping strategy to fend off the world might look like the answer. Yet strategies require memorization and calculated action. They won't free your mind—they'll only add more clutter. Knowing how the mind works, however, clarifies the source of your feelings and points you inside. It allows your psychological immune system (stale-thinking-out/fresh-thinking-in) to heal any momentary glitch.

The choice is yours: Understand the system and then calmly find answers. Or panic and apply shots in the dark.

Interestingly enough, this understanding is at the core of great leadership, too.

THE DIFFERENCE BETWEEN LEADERSHIP AND MOTIVATION

Reflect for a moment on those people who have sparked the pilot light inside you and influenced your life in an inspiring way. I pose this request here, with just a little time left on the clock, for a reason. I hope you'll respond differently than you would have if you had not read this book. Still to this day, old friends and teammates of mine find it hard to believe that a man with a ninth-grade education who never played a sport in his life, Sydney Banks, is at the top of my list of inspiring people. So is my grandmother, who lived and gave to others until the age of one hundred. And so are the true leaders I've mentioned throughout these pages: Martin Luther King Jr., Nelson Mandela, Abraham Lincoln, Mother Teresa, and others.

I'll tell you about another top-notch leader. You know her by now. Her name is Elizabeth (Liz) Kramer, my wife, and she leads without effort.

To depict her leadership skill, I'll share a note that Liz secretly tucked into my briefcase. I found it right in the middle of writing this book, at a time when my thoughts about the project were filled with doubt:

> Babe,
>
> I'm so proud of you. Nobody knows better than you that we all question ourselves sometimes. Stay in the game. I believe in you, and what you have to say to others. . . .

She closed with something I won't share, but the note rings quiet and clear: Inspiring leaders don't suggest methods to put into practice, or things to do, in order to assist others. (Okay, she reminded me to stay in the game, but we both know what that means.) Rather, inspiring leaders support and take interest. Liz said she believed in me and that she was proud. She turned me away from the normal ups and downs of my thinking about writing a book (a circumstance) and inward toward the book's purpose. This purpose is the foundation for every remarkable thing that any person has ever done. Leaders guide others to their ability to self-correct. Leaders guide others to love.

As I said, the possibilities are boundless when a person, such as Liz in this example, grasps the thought-feeling connection. Like all consistent and industrious people, inspiring leaders seem to know how the system works; it rarely occurs to them to look outside to explain how anyone (including themselves) feels on the inside.

Here's another feature of leadership, and it's almost always confused today: Leadership and motivation are not the same thing. In fact, people in leadership positions who try to light fires for others rarely have a lasting impact. They also tend to not keep their jobs for very long.

The difference between leadership and motivation can be summed up like this:

Leadership: *Setting a consistent example of rising above circumstance. Leadership is external.*

Motivation: *The inner knowledge or insight that makes rising above circumstance possible. Motivation comes from within.*

So, genuine leadership isn't necessarily about encouraging, pushing, or cheering on; it's not about suggesting practices or behaviors. It's about showing others that motivation rests within them.

If you're a parent, for instance, you know that it's virtually impossible to prod your children to work hard at their studies. But you can lead. No matter what life throws at you or how difficult your circumstances appear, you can passionately apply yourself to your own job or projects. Thereby pointing your children to their own innate ability to rise above any circumstance, or excuse, and crack the books with pride and vigor.

This book's slant on leadership is simple: Real leaders serve to bring out the inner wisdom and free will of those they serve. Instead of inducing people to view life situations a certain way—or their way—real leaders prove that there are endless ways to view any life situation. Sydney Banks gave hundreds of lectures during his lifetime. However, he always asked his audiences not to take notes. He wanted them to invoke their own views and draw their own conclusions, not follow in his footsteps. Now that's a leader.

This doesn't mean that leaders don't strive to get their point across or fervently stand behind their opinions. They do. But while they burn to succeed, leaders never live at the mercy of success (or of anything external). Go back to our field-goal kicker. If he misses the kick, he and his team will be down, but not out. Possibilities always exist.

The bottom line on leadership? Leaders set inspiring examples born from clarity and understanding. So why not leave leadership right there? Who ever came up with the credo that leaders must be motivators anyway? Isn't it time we recognize the difference between leadership and motivation? Because if we don't, our companies, teams, schools, and families will be overrun by followers who aren't capable of lending an imaginative hand, let alone making prudent decisions when the chips are down.

Motivation is personal. Leadership brings out one's personal potential for the welfare of the greater good. Let's get to know the difference. The business, sports, education, and political worlds—actually the world in general—can use more of both.

EFFECTIVE COMMUNICATION: THE TRUTH

One other comment about inspiring leaders: Believe it or not, when they speak, they don't pay much attention to the words that come out of their mouths. They know that the level of consciousness from which their words are spoken will, or will not, make a positive difference for others.

Me, I've tried it both ways when it comes to communication. In preparing for talks, I've written out notes and rehearsed (an approach I haven't tried for years). But I've also walked onstage and spoken from my heart and intuition. The difference? My talks were far more eloquent when

I had no idea what I was going to say next. When I spoke without thinking, the feeling in the room was tremendous.

Yet, every day we hear more and more experts, in just about every field of endeavor, stressing the need for effective communication. Or that communication, in and of itself, is critical. These experts might say, "For a person, organization, or marriage to achieve long-term success, communication is key." Or, I'm sure you've heard this type of warning: "A lack of communication is why relationships fall apart."

After I wrote my first book, my publisher jumped on this bandwagon, too. The publishing team wanted me to take a class on communicating my message. Sure, they meant to help. But contaminating my own thinking with someone else's way to converse was not going to help me deliver my message.

As backward as it might seem, one reason projects often fail, unions dissolve, or teams lose is because people *over-communicate*. They force interaction. They speak when they're not capable of doing so productively (because their heads are filled with thought). The art of communication is obvious and natural. Want a class on communication? Look to your feelings.

To demonstrate, say a lawyer finds herself in a bad mood after a long day in court. She comes home, tired and hungry, and just wants to take a hot bath and have a glass of wine before dinner. But her husband, a writer and stay-at-home dad, had a long day, too. He got nowhere on the first chapter of his new book, was late picking up the kids from school, and didn't have time to prepare dinner.

Yet, rather than grasping that her feelings and perception of this circumstance are the byproduct of her own mood and staying silent, the lawyer unloads: "I thought we had an agreement when I went back to work. I support you and your writing; you take care of our home, and that includes dinner!"

And why not? The lawyer is convinced, like many, that the secret to effective communication is speaking your mind honestly and freely. The night spirals downward from there.

On the other side of this communication conundrum is the subject of listening. It's regularly argued that effective communication doesn't only revolve around talking; more significant, it revolves around listening. That's not always the case. When feeling insecure, the last thing a person should do is lend an ear to any external source. Why? We've talked about it before. Insecurity breeds the desire to latch on to another person's methodology or line of thinking, to become a follower. Do you remember the sordid tale of Jim Jones and Jonestown? Regrettably, Jones's devotees listened perfectly to their cult founder.

No question: Communication is important, but not as a strategy for enhancing your performance, relationships, mood, or life. We mustn't worry about speaking our minds or keeping an open mind (listening). We must only consider the state of mind from which we do these things. This, in fact, explains why many of the world's most effective leaders are quite reticent. They understand that if they speak from insecurity—a place from which they aren't seeing life clearly—they're bound to do so in error. Plus, if they listen from an insecure state, they might adopt someone else's wayward point of view (thus explaining Nazi Germany and the formation of every terrorist organization the world has ever known).

Danger lurks if you look outside and communicate, or act, when you're suffering. With free will blocked, nobody stands a chance.

———————

Here, on a lighter note, is an amusing personal story about effective discourse. One night last year, I arrived home out of sorts after a long day (much like our lawyer). Liz did have dinner on the table, but it was meatballs, a meal that didn't agree with my tastes or diet (or so I thought). As a result of my low level of consciousness, I started in, "Why in the world would you make meatballs when I'm trying to reduce my red meat intake?"

To which Liz insightfully replied, "Not. Listening."

Translation: Liz detected my lack of clarity and instead of taking the bait, she refused to communicate. My response: I immediately snapped out of my funk, stopped talking, and quietly sat down to dinner. A dinner of *turkey* meatballs and gravy—how scrumptious!

AN OPTICAL ILLUSION

You see, circling back to leadership, Liz is a tactfully good leader. The meatball incident is a surprising example of effective communication, or an effective lack of communication, but it's also an example of leading another person inward. One of the most rewarding aspects of my work is knowing that when people move inward for answers, innate resilience and thus leadership become reliable constants.

Are you familiar with the saying "Leaders aren't born; they're made"? I disagree with it. Leadership is not consigned to a select hard-working few in this world. Everyone's a born leader. Including you. Just be you; that's all it takes. If this book serves the mere purpose of fostering your instincts, determination, and compassion for others—in your own way—then I'm beyond psyched. And proud, of us both.

As we make our way to the finish line (and don't miss the afterword and the appendix filled with my favorite personal quotes), here's a final portrayal of the path of no resistance in action. Through the eyes of a close friend, it reveals what's possible when we look away from circumstance, stay in the game, and turn toward our innate resilience.

My buddy Joe Bier once called me with a question about the inside-out paradigm. He asked: "Every time I see my grandchildren, I feel good inside. Are you telling me that my grandchildren are not the cause of my good mood?"

I said, "Yes, that's what I'm telling you."

"It sure feels and looks like you're wrong," he countered.

Well, as you know by now, I do agree with Joe about how it often *appears* that our circumstances are responsible for what we feel. But as my wise colleague Gina Woolf once told me:

> *Life works from the inside-out 100 percent of the time—not 99 percent. So we know with certainty that when it looks like something outside is causing us to feel (fill in the blank), that's just the optical illusion of our thinking making a case for something that's never true no matter how much it feels and looks like it is.*

In other words, while there's a correlation between Joe's grandchildren and his feeling state, as with umbrella usage and storm-sewer overflow (George Pransky's illustration mentioned in chapter 4), there is not a causal relationship. And understanding this distinction is an essential ingredient in activating your innate ability to find clarity and live a productive life moving forward.

So, let's dig just a little bit deeper before we close up shop.

Here, to me, is how visiting his grandchildren really plays out for Joe (and you can compare Joe's experience to any experience of your own): On days that Joe's head is clear and he's feeling good, he goes to see his grandchildren and his good mood continues. Simple.

But the cool thing about Joe is that on days when he has a lot on his mind and doesn't feel good, he stays in the game and still sees his grandchildren anyway. And because he does this, his head clears.

However—and this is super-important to point out again—it's not seeing his grandchildren that clears Joe's head. What brings Joe clarity is the fact that he doesn't delve into all the outside factors that seem to be bothering him. Joe looks away from his apparent business issues, the traffic, the weather, whatever—and automatically finds himself in a better mood. Yes, his grandchildren are adorable. But Joe can go anywhere or do anything, other than think into his troubles, and regulate to peace of mind.

Never forget: It works the same for you.

It may appear as if an external action or environment (going to see your grandchildren, performing a mental strategy, watching a movie, taking a walk on the beach, practicing yoga) has the power to alter your mind-set. But it's never the case.

Everyone lives in the feeling of their thinking, not the feeling of their circumstances, right? So if you feel down and look outside to explain or excuse why, paralysis by analysis will set in. But if, like Joe, you look inside and get on with your day, your psychological immune system will intercede and you will feel better. Resilience, excellence, and love will then start to emerge because life works one way only—from the inside-out.

Now, as we cross the finish line, let's take a final peek at the thought-feeling connection, and the strength and simplicity of looking within.

SIMPLICITY AS YOU GO

For me, the utmost challenge in all of my work is that I'm attempting to explain the unexplainable. *The Path of No Resistance*, in essence, describes a spiritual process that's beyond description. So at those moments when my insecurity crept in over the past few months (as it did when Liz put the note in my briefcase), I just kept writing, using the words the dictionary provides. All the while praying that I wasn't complicating the most basic understanding known to mankind. Many people (and I've referred to several) do inadvertently complicate it. I believe it's my responsibility to do better.

Paying attention to this responsibility, I revealed something significant early in this book: Originally, psychology was the study of the mind and soul. But because we didn't appreciate the spiritual simplicity of our inner wisdom and innate functioning, psychology was converted to the study of behavior. We've been reeling in this reversed direction ever since.

Today's institutions of higher learning, unfortunately, are no exception to this outward focus. In their desire to instill independence or self-sufficiency in their students (as if you could ever do such a thing), universities are complicating personal development that's meant to be intuitive. Here's an e-mail from a top liberal arts college in the US to the parents of incoming freshman students:

> Please feel free to call the office of the Dean of Student Affairs with any parent-specific questions you might have. But we request that you do not solicit questions on behalf of your freshman students. The time is now for them to start advocating for themselves.

How does this directive strike you? Parents dole out heaps of cash for their son or daughter to attend college, and then with no cause whatsoever, these parents are told how to behave. If anyone should know about the self-defeating quality of outside-in (that if anything, it adds thought and worry, which ups the odds that the parents *will* call on their student's behalf), it's the administration of liberal arts colleges. As we've found out, students will naturally learn to advocate for themselves at the proper place and time—if we don't interfere.

This is why knowing how the mind works, and not predicting, judging, or addressing behavior, is so imperative. Yes, we can rise above anything. But, as William James and Sydney Banks warned many years ago, behavior modification is a tall mountain to climb. Mix inner wisdom with external orders and one's thought system tends to race. Then behavior gets fickle.

Even so, the college's edict and all other external circumstances remain neutral. Parents, students, and all: You're not forced to follow jumbled thoughts and unsettled feelings, if you have them. That's the reason I wrote this book.

Actually, understanding the source of our inner sensations is the baseline for all aspects of my work. For instance, one thing I do professionally is interview and assess prospective athletes for pro teams before draft day. Every year, based on their order of finish in the standings, teams pick college or amateur athletes to join their rosters. If a team is interested in a player, I'm asked to give my opinion on the player's mental makeup. Most other assessments of this kind involve administering multiple-choice tests, which often take hours. My test, however, is far simpler and takes five minutes at most. It consists of one basic question for the prospect:

What causes a person's troubles?

That's all you need to ask to gauge a player's potential—and level of consciousness or understanding. Is the answer a person's circumstance, environment, or past? Or does the answer rest inside the person, in his or her thinking? Is a person's life all over the place? Or is a person's thinking all over the place and just getting the better of him or her at that moment? As you can see, revealing questions and answers are elementary, if you know where to find them.

In fact, our first step down the path of no resistance was

an elementary question: What do we really observe, and then experience, as we look outward? On our way to the answer, we explored every conceivable aspect of our inborn ability to rise above. We delved into the principle of thought, the notion of inside-out, the purpose of feelings, the necessity of staying in the game, and the universal power of love. All of this was done to illustrate the freeing paradigm that each of us lives in the feeling of our thinking, not in the feeling of what happens to us in the world outside.

Along the path, I also asked you to solve this riddle: Why has no one ever told you about the thought-feeling connection, yet at the same time you know it to be true?

Got it solved?

If not, it's okay. Don't try as hard and you'll see: This book hasn't said one thing that, deep down, you didn't already know. Equally important, there isn't a shred of information here that must be studied, memorized, or practiced. Your only job is to let truth go to work—on you.

In writing *The Path of No Resistance,* my hope has always been this: to affirm that circumstances can't lead to success or failure. Or love or hate. It's only something within you— your thinking—that does this. So perhaps, from here on out, you'll stop perpetuating problems that have nothing to do with your feelings and allow your mind to self-correct. Looking outside creates frustration. Looking inside creates clarity. No matter what.

I also hope this book has shown that when a person

glances away from the world of form, and toward the spiritual wisdom within, anything is possible. I'm living proof. And so are you. No person is more spiritual or more privileged than anyone else. The path is one and the same for everyone. Our experience of struggle is merely a reflection of the thoughts that randomly pop into our heads and, if we don't feed them with attention and belief, will just as easily pop out.

Above all, remember this as you go: Resilience, like happiness, won't be found in someone else's methods, concepts, or ideals. Resilience is innate. The reason you can overcome anything is because, in truth, there's nothing you need to overcome. Get out there and live life on your own terms, knowing that when you do feel low, fretting and fixing are not mandatory—or beneficial.

When you get right down to it, overcoming is as natural as breathing. Overcoming is simple.

AFTERWORD:
SEVEN INSIDE–OUT KEYS TO OVERCOMING

Together, we've covered the entire path of no resistance as I see it at this moment. But that'll change. There's no end to insight and possibility. We're forever learning; there's always room for consciousness to grow.

It can't be forced to grow, mind you. Simply consider: What are the implications of the paradigm introduced in this book for you, your family, your community, and the world? Then go get 'em. When lived from the inside-out, productivity has a way of taking care of itself.

One topic we covered is the fundamental fact that we live in a world of form. As a result, everyone is prone to occasional upsets or disappointments. There are far more participants than champions in the sports world, for example, and not every relationship is destined for a lifelong commitment. While this book has detailed why some people handle failure and go on to prosper, and why it seems to scar others for life, I think there's merit in taking a closing look.

If you ever get stuck and need a soft nudge inward, the following inside-out resilience refreshers might come in handy. They always work for me.

1. *You cannot control your thinking.*

   The human mind is designed to effortlessly replace stale thinking with insight. If you obstruct this process by trying to look on the bright side (think positively), you'll perpetuate struggle and confusion.

2. *Keep goal setting in perspective.*

   Focusing on goals stifles the ever-changing nature of your thinking. That's why if you set goals and don't reach them, disappointment will fester. Even though they might feel down in the moment, those who overcome failure recognize that all outcomes are opportunities for growth, new possibilities, and future success.

3. *External circumstances are neutral.*

   Why is it that one moment we can be distraught about a circumstance like losing, and the next moment look at the same circumstance and wonder why we were upset in the first place? The reason is that, in principle, outside events are neutral (you don't feel your circumstances). Realize this and you can overcome anything.

4. *Your reality is created from the inside-out.*

Your experience doesn't create your state of mind; your state of mind creates your experience. It's okay to feel upset if you don't win, but those who learn from the experience of losing know that their thinking, and not the loss itself, is the cause of the upset. The loss remains (at least on paper), but your thinking and perspective are guaranteed to change.

5. *Your feelings are your guide.*

Again, there's nothing wrong with you if you can't shake a disappointment. But remember: The "off" feeling in your gut is an intuitive sign that your thinking and perceptions are off-kilter. Those who prosper from defeat know better than to fight through momentary lacks of clarity.

6. *From a low mood, distrust your thinking.*

From a low state of mind, your thinking is never helpful—or true. The simple secret to rising above failure is to not believe what you think when this type of mood sets in.

7. *Stay in the game.*

What happens when you sit on the sidelines and think yourself into a troublesome experience? It grows and grows. Strategically pausing to figure out or fix a dysfunctional mind-set only holds dysfunction in place. Rather, the key to overcoming adversity is to stay in the game and allow your psychological immune system to clear the dysfunction. Answers will then find you. Success or failure, every experience is guiding you inward—where resilience truly rests.

Thanks for reading. Here's hoping our paths cross one day soon.

APPENDIX:
A LIST OF MY OWN QUOTATIONS

The purpose of the following long list of my own quotes and anecdotes is to reinforce the principles revealed in *The Path of No Resistance*. Please feel free to share.

- Any judgment, theory, assumption, or belief that comes from your ability to think (since it's subject to change) is not real. Love is the only thing that doesn't come from your ability to think. Love is the only thing that's real.

- When analyzing an achievement, people often look at the steps taken as opposed to the clarity and wisdom that created the steps. There's no road map to excellence.

- Grasping that struggles stem from thought, and not circumstance, is what allows the self-corrective nature of the mind to spring into action.

- Instead of convincing team members to view situations a certain way (or their way), great leaders demonstrate that there are an infinite number of ways to view any situation.

- Coaches, I get it. Many players don't think they can win, notably when they get close to beating a favored rival. But here's the thing: They don't have to think they can win. They have to be able to win, no matter what they are thinking. To do that, players must first understand the randomness and neutrality of thought.

- Life is productive when you get caught up in the experience; unproductive when you make the experience about you.

- If performance results (statistics, championships, awards) matter to you more than the overall experience of being alive—both will suffer.

- Those who delve into the past to explain current troubles are seeking answers in the same sea of misinformation that created their troubles in the first place.

- Obstacles are figments of your thinking. That's why as soon as your old thinking departs, new thinking arrives and obstacles fade away.

- Application versus understanding:

  Application: When I was young and someone told me what to do to raise my low mood, I would apply the strategy, feel better for a minute, and then feel even worse.

  Understanding: Now I understand that trying to fix my low moods doesn't work, so I don't do it anymore and my lows are short-lived.

- Contrary to what most of us think, there's not a conclusive link between external demands and internal stress.

- What most therapists and mediators overlook is that in any struggling relationship, the "issues" are the effect of the dysfunction—never the cause.

- You're under no obligation to treat the thoughts that pop into your head as true.

- Sports commentators often talk about pitch counts and protecting the arms of young baseball pitchers. Yes, biology, kinesiology, and data are relevant factors. But don't lose sight of this: Pitchers in a calm and quiet mind-set naturally conserve energy— so they can throw more pitches without getting injured.

- Using a technique to find "the zone" is like using witchcraft to make the sun rise.

- The gap between believing that your circumstances create your feelings and realizing that your thinking creates your feelings will determine your level of contentment. The narrower the gap, the more content you'll be; the wider the gap, the less.

- Negative thoughts are not a problem for any of us at any time. Acting on these thoughts—such as trying to manage them—is a different story.

- If you're tempted to do something and feel "off," then, rest assured, doing it won't make you feel better.

- An expert on the *Today* show once claimed that when you're angry you should stop and think before you react. Hmm, an angry person is supposed to add more thought to his or her already frenzied thought system. How do you think that'll work out?

- Peace of mind is not a state of perpetual bliss. It's knowing that when you feel low, there's nothing to fret about; nothing is broken.

- Gratitude is a momentary experience that has little to do with people, things, or events.

- Listening, and its importance, is often discussed. But like knowing when to speak, knowing when to listen is also key. Listening from an insecure mind-set has contributed to more conflict than we can count—from family turmoil, to bullying, to terrorism, to world wars.

- Actual problems exist both when your mood is bad and when it's good. Now, how many problems do you actually have?

- Employing a mental strategy and then feeling better is called coincidence. Getting on with life and then self-correcting is called truth.

- Having trouble forgiving others? Don't fuss. Just realize that forgiveness is not about someone else. When your level of well-being is high, forgiveness is automatic. When low, nearly impossible.

- Do you think there's a connection between a life event and your feelings? If yes, wait a bit, then look again.

- A high school triple-jumper from New Jersey soared to number two in the nation with a jump of 49 feet, 7.5 inches. Afterward, a young boy came up to the jumper and asked him what he thinks about when he's jumping. His reply: "That's a pretty strange question; I don't have an answer for you." Exactly. People find excellence through an absence of thought. Why aren't performance coaches connecting the dots? They keep prescribing mental techniques that require people to think.

- The holidays are wonderful. Just keep in mind: Gratitude, compassion, and love are generated from inside of you. The calendar has no power over your thinking.

- In any relationship, if winning is what you're after, you'll lose 100 percent of the time.

- For many, the problem with the past is not what's happened. It's whether or not they understand that their judgment of what's happened is solely determined by their present thinking.

- Since respectful competition often leads to success, remember this whenever you face a foe on the playing field: Through competition, everyone grows. (I push you to get better; you push me.) Both sides are working together to expand their capabilities, knowledge, and consciousness.

- Do you know folks who are so concerned about negative thoughts that they resort to strategies to change them? They don't understand how insignificant the content of their thinking really is.

- If nothing else, the scandal at Penn State University involving sexual abuse and wide-scale cover-up shows us that adhering to the edicts of a culture binds a person's thinking, obstructs free will, and creates followers who are incapable of coming through in the big moment.

- Consider this as you find yourself rushing around: You don't have to do anything. Okay, go ahead and list all the things you think you have to do. Then, see it all as thought and watch how the rushing disappears.

- Nine out of ten people would say that behavior born from insecurity is not beneficial. So in the US, perhaps we're looking at the heated gun debate from the wrong direction. To me, it's not the behavior of buying a gun that's the issue. Doing this or anything from a disposition of insecurity (or fear) is why all hell breaks loose.

- Are you holding a grudge? Most will tell you it's wrong to do so, but not me. Instead, be guided by your answer to this question: How do you feel while holding a grudge? Cool and composed, or desperate and bound up?

- Your perception of life, including how you view the actions of others, has nothing to do with what takes place in life. It's determined by your own thoughts, feelings, and subsequent state of mind—at this very moment.

- We often forget that our troubles are caused by our thinking. So we use our thinking to solve our troubles—causing more troubles.

- Rule number one: If you disagree with another person and feel upset, there's not much you should do about it. Rule number two: If you're blaming the other person for your upset feelings, it's you who isn't seeing things quite right.

- People don't miss opportunities because they're too focused on obstacles. They miss opportunities because they're too focused.

- How do you know if the time is right to deviate from a plan? Hint: If you're wondering, the time isn't right.

- Let's stop using "a lack of interest in the things that one's usually passionate about" as a sign of depression. It's a sign of the normal fluctuations of a person's thinking.

- Effort, or doing your best, is not the same thing as grinding, or trying your hardest.

- In the fields of politics, sports, coaching, teaching, and parenting, we need fewer historians and more trailblazers. Abraham Lincoln was a trailblazer; Jackie Robinson was a trailblazer; Sydney Banks was a trailblazer.

- At the root of all problems lies a person who bought into the distorted vision of his or her temporarily low mind-set.

- Free will isn't possible if you believe or try to control the thoughts that occur to you.

- Most of us recognize that our thinking and moods fluctuate. Yet, we overlook that our perceptions of life follow right along.

- Goal setting blocks imagination, limits awareness, and prevents possibilities. Besides, your level of self-worth has nothing to do with whether you reach a particular goal, or not.

- There's a big difference between the feeling of sadness (a productive emotion born from love) and the feeling of misery (a destructive emotion born from a passing low psychological perspective).

- Discord with another person isn't possible unless you are both operating from a low state of mind.

- Negative feelings are normal, necessary, and possess an often-overlooked positive. They're an instinctive sign that your thinking, not your life, is off course. In other words, negative feelings say look inward or risk steering into trouble.

- Admitting that there are many ways to think about the same situation is a sign that a "difficult" situation will correct itself soon.

- If a friend is in need, it's never a good idea to identify with his or her issue. Why? Because you'll drop to your friend's level of discontent and won't be able to help. Rather, provide compassion and support. They always work better than commiseration and sympathy.

- Growth only occurs when learning is approached from an impersonal perspective. You can't make things personal and have an open and clear mind at the same time.

- The degree to which athletes and coaches understand that external circumstances have no ability to regulate performance will determine their ability to execute in the clutch.

- When offering advice or instruction to someone, your words will always pale in comparison to the state of mind from which they are spoken.

- Trying to avoid an unwanted experience is the quickest way to have an unwanted experience.

- Have you ever noticed that the most stressed-out people are constantly doing "something" to fend off stress?

- I heard on talk radio that people who tell fewer lies live longer. Makes sense. But then the reporter went on: People who tell fewer lies have better relationships, and people with better relationships live longer. No. People live longer, have better relationships, and tell fewer lies because they live in a higher state of consciousness than those who live shorter lives, have poor relationships, and tell many lies. Inside-out, people, not outside-in.

- Linking feelings to circumstance is a common and unbreakable habit. How often you dodge this habit will establish your level of clarity, joy, fortitude, and efficiency.

- A secret to resilience? Not grinding away, but knowing that perspective and emotion shift naturally without effort.

- You'll never find happiness by delving into your unhappiness.

- There's no connection between performance excellence and positive thinking. Stop trying to find a state of no thought by adding thought!

- I felt stressed, instinctively took a deep breath, and then felt better. So, what was the stress reliever—deep breathing or my instincts?

- Problems aren't the cause of disquiet. They're a symptom of it:
  Situation + disquiet mind-set = problem
  Same situation + tranquil mind-set = no problem

- While thoughts are powerful enough to produce errant feelings, they are not powerful enough to produce errant behaviors.

- Are you battling to keep up? The answer is never to speed up.

- If you're a coach and need to create competition within your team to bring out the best in your players, you've got two issues: 1. You're coaching the wrong players. 2. You don't understand where a player's best originates.

- Regardless of different backgrounds, intelligence,

or personalities, everyone's struggles come from the same place: their thinking.

- Free will doesn't mean that you shouldn't listen to the advice of another. It means that you shouldn't follow it blindly.

- People who try to control their thoughts will not produce consistently; they'll only produce consistently revved-up thoughts.

- Attempting to fix a predicament and feeling worse? That's because you're trying to fix something that once your mind settles won't exist.

- Emotion is instinctual. Analyzing emotion is learned.

- It's impossible to outsmart, outhustle, or willfully change your current feeling state. When you're in a low place and not thinking clearly, the trick is to lighten up on the gas pedal and drive steadily on— not to press it harder.

- The brain is biological, the mind pure spirit.

- Imagine the confusion: You know that your feelings are coming from the inside, but it sure looks like they're coming from the outside. Welcome to the human race.

- I've heard ample opinions about shunning certain people in life. I disagree. For a better life, do the opposite.

- Peace of mind takes no work at all. If you're working, you're cluttering—and complicating.

- Never out to in. Experience does not create state of mind. State of mind creates experience.

- There's only one way to truly inspire others: No matter the challenge, remain inspired yourself.

- Self-help is an interesting word. How can employing someone else's motivational or mental strategy really be self-help?

- When thought fills your head, life looks bleak. When thought empties, life looks beautiful. Believe the beautiful.

- A client once said to me, "It's nice to finally talk to someone who doesn't interfere with my psychological immune system." Music to my ears.

- The path of no resistance begins and ends with love.

ACKNOWLEDGMENTS

Overcoming may be simple. Writing a book about it, well, it wasn't too bad, especially since I had the support of so many.

Kristina Holmes, my agent and friend. Your advice is always direct, on point, and, at the same time, compassionate and caring. The true sign of an inside-out perspective. To Clint Greenleaf and his entire team, thank you for believing in me and in the principles that guide my message. My pal Sherry Roberts had the unenviable task of cleaning up my dangling participles and the like. Her editing brought clarity to my words. Yoori Kim provided the perfect artwork for the jacket of this book before the project was even a quarter complete. Intuitive minds think alike, Yoori, even from halfway around the world.

To my colleagues, Jamie Smart, Chantal Burns, Michael Neill, Keith Blevens, Gina Woolf, Don Donovan, and George Pransky: My appreciation for what we teach, and the collaboration between us, knows no bounds. The late

Richard Carlson was the person who introduced me to the work of Sydney Banks. Words cannot adequately describe my fondness for them both.

As luck would have it, I fell into writing this book during the winter months. Meaning, I didn't miss either of my sons' college baseball games, or my daughter's field hockey or lacrosse games. I was pretty much unavailable, however, during the book's writing. So, to my three amazing children—Ryan, Jackson, and Chelsea, to whom *The Path of No Resistance* is dedicated—I love you to the moon and back, and owe you some quality time as well.

Finally, my greatest gratitude, by far, is reserved for the person who entertained every random idea that popped into my head, read the book's manuscript numerous times, listened to me read it out loud, and kept all external circumstances at bay as I stayed in the game—Elizabeth Kramer. Who knew, sweetheart, that when we spoke on the phone twenty-six years ago over chocolate-chip-mint ice cream, we had *truly* found the path of no resistance.

INDEX

A

Acceptance, 66–68
Achievement, 189
Actions
 being upset over another's, 233
 hateful, 175–176
 from love, 161
Acuity gap, 31–33, 80, 230
Advice, offering, 237
Alcohol use, 11, 116, 150, 156
Allen, Woody, 123
Anger, 62, 230
Anti-bullying protocols, 81
Antonoff, Jack, xiii
Anxiety, 7, 105, 137
Application versus understanding,
 203–207, 229
Arrogance, from overthinking, 183
Awareness
 limitations of, 235
 practicing, 66, 95
 reducing, 111, 133, 155

B

Bamberger, Michael, 11
Banks, Sydney, 13, 14–15, 18, 19,
 41, 70, 79, 123, 138, 159,
 178, 191, 208, 210, 219,
 235
Baseball, performance-enhancing
 drug scandals in, 56–57
Batt, Greg, 99, 100, 127
Beatles, 79
Behavior
 cause and effect of problems in,
 16–19
 focusing on, 12–13
 insecurity as born from, 233
 psychological principles behind,
 16
Believing, 196–199
Bhasker, Jeff, xiii
Bier, Joe, 215–217
Blevens, Keith, 5, 13n
Blumenfeld, Jay, 162–165

Bound-up feelings, 207
Bound-up thinking, 69, 173
Braudy, Susan, 123n
Brian's Song, 203
Brickman, Philip, 60n
Bullying, 12, 81–83, 84, 150, 231

C

Calmness, inexplicable, 105–109
Caring, 169–171
Carlson, Richard, 5, 197
Carrey, Jim, 60
Cause and effect of behavioral
        problems, 16–19
Central nervous system, alignment
        and workings of the, 103
Change
        constant, in outlook, 3
        of perspective and emotion, 237
        making happen, 95–99
Charity, 183
Cheating, 56–58
Childhood, ability to hurt, 69–70
Children
        being hung up on thinking,
                23–25
        counseling, 185
        discipline of, 185
        fretting about one's, 85
        pigeonholing with haphazard
                opinions and diagnoses,
                185
        secret of, to resilience, inspira-
                tion, and happiness, 23
Circumstances
        blaming, 63

confronting and overcoming, 2
experiencing, 1–2
feeling and, 21–22
neutrality of external, 224
perceptions of, 3
power of, 38
tie of thinking to, 20–21
Clarity, 183
        lack of, 113, 125
        resisting, 4
        waiting from, 125, 227
*Clarity: Clear Mind, Better
        Performance, Bigger Results*
        (Smart), 170, 128n
Coates, Dan, 60n
Codes of conduct, 12, 81, 147, 148,
        187
Coincidence, 87
Colvin, Geoff, 132–134, 135
Communication
        and listening, 213, 214
        stress on, 188
        truth about, 211–214
Compassion, 63, 80, 169, 181, 183,
        215, 232, 236
        as foundation of inner wisdom,
                165
Competition
        as cooperation in disguise,
                179–180
        respectful, 232
Confidence, dealing with lack of,
        36–37
Conflict, 231
Consciousness
        defined, xi

love and respect as symptoms of, 186
principles of, 5, 14
Contempt, environment of, 179
Cooperation, 180
Coping mechanisms, 2, 31, 207
Correlation, cause and effect and, 135
Crisis, avoiding, 90–92
Culture, endorsing, 188

D
Deci, Edward, 156
Deep-breathing/visualization technique, 137
Deliberate practice, 134
theory of, 132–133
Depression, 70
reasons for, 74–76
signs of, 234
Dialing it down, 127–128
Discipline, 185
threats of, 58
Disconcerted thinking, 196
Disconnect, 25–27
Discourse, effective, 214
Disingenuousness, 113–114
Disrespect, 64, 164, 175–176, 187, 190
Distorted perceptions, 78, 235
Distractions, 7
Distrust of thinking, 18, 225
Divorce, prevalence of, 175
Don't Sweat the Small Stuff (Carlson), 197
Dost, Andrew, xiii

Drive: The Surprising Truth About What Motivates Us (Pink), 156–157
Drugs
performance-enhancing, 56–57
use of, 11, 116–118
Dysfunction, effect of, 229
Dysfunctional thoughts, 32, 81, 97, 117

E
Efficiency, 90, 183
Effort, 235
driving, with freedom, 189
Ego, 56, 117
environment of, 179
Empirical evidence, 195
Employers, forcing of belief systems on employees, 45
Energy
conserving, 229
flow of, 103–105
formless, 178
Excellence, natural bond between love and, 169
Exercise, 12
Expectations, 58
limiting, 187
setting, 150–152, 160
Experience
illusion of pressure and, 49–51
nature of, 1–2
psychological perspective of, 18
quality of, 2
true source of human, 159
varying, 3

External circumstances, neutrality
of, 224
External demands, internal stress
and, 229

F

Failure, 51, 61, 94, 187
Fearful thinking, 27
Federer, Roger, 74–75
Feelings
bound-up, 207
change of, 239
controlling, 202–203
defined, xi
as guide, 124, 225
as impossible to ignore, 88
inborn purpose of, 97–99
as life-indicator, 76
listening to your, 116
as magic bullet, 90
paradoxical purpose of, 120
reasons for low, 74–78
reliability of, 114–118
of uncertainty, 123–124
up-and-down flow of, 99
Feeling state, defined, xii
Fired, being, 176
Fix-it technique, 138
Flay, Bobby, 74–75
Fortitude, innate, 2
Freedom, driving effort with, 189
Free-flowing thought, 27
Free will, 20, 23, 45, 136, 186, 188,
233, 235, 239
inherent functioning and, 151
promoting, 59, 185

success and, 146–149
Fulfillment, quest for, 64

G

Galileo, 13
Gandhi, Mahatma, 178
Gladwell, Malcolm, 132, 134, 135
Goals
love and, 160
setting, 150–158, 160, 235
keeping in perspective, 224
keeping to minimum, 186
God, defining, 159, 160
Grahl, Tim, 129–130, 137
Gratitude, 230, 232
Grind-it-out paradigm, 189
Grudges, 23, 233

H

Hang-ups, 184
Happiness, 58–62, 238, 239
collective level of, 184
practicing, 66
quest for, 179
resisting, 4
The Happiness Project (Rubin), 59
Hard work, 99–102
as foundation of success, 134
Harlow, Harry, 156
Hate, 187
love, respect, and togetherness as
simpler sentiments than,
178
misdirection of, 175–177
Hoosiers, 93
Hours-applied rule, 135

Hughes, Phil, 107–109

Human experience, inside-outness of, 44

Hurricane Katrina, rebuilding after, 155

Hurricane Sandy
    dealing with, 121–122
    lessons on principle of thought, 181–183

Hurt, passage of time in erasing, 119–120

Hypnosis, 12

I

Illness, focusing on, 64–65

Illusionary past, 69–71

Imagination
    being guided by, 153
    goal setting in blocking, 235

Incentives, failing of external, 156

Incompetence from overthinking, 183

Inconsistency, steadiness versus, 94

Indecision, 92

Individuality, recognizing and embracing, 186

Inherent functioning, free will and, 151

Inhibitions, 184

Innate fortitude, 2

Innate reflexes, overriding, 25

Innate resilience, Olympic excellence and, 34–37

Inner peace
    level of, 2
    retaining, 6

Inner sensation, source of our, 220

Inner Sports, 5

Inner wisdom, 165
    detaching oneself from, 6
    listening to, 4

Innovative ideas in waking up organization, 186–189

Insecurity, 63, 87, 117, 182, 213
    behavior born from, 233
    reinforcing, 110

Inside-out, 43–78
    acceptance and, 66–68
    as all-encompassing, 74
    cheating and, 56–58
    creation of reality from, 5, 225
    defined, xii
    experiencing life from, 43
    forming perceptions and, 20
    grasping meaning of, 197–198
    happiness and, 58–62
    illusionary past and, 69–71
    illusion of pressure and experience, 49–51
    innate potential and, 54–56
    intuitive signs of low state of mind, 62–66
    looking at mental health through lens of, 80–81
    versus outside-in, 133
    passion pursuit and, 52–53
    reasons for feeling low, 74–78
    as source of human experience, 159
    time and state of mind, 71–73
    understanding, 161–163
    working of, 97–99

Inside-out paradigm, 194, 215
  components of, 67–68
The Inside-Out Revolution (Neill), 89
Insight
  defined, xi
  difference between worry and,
    84–87
  replacing stale thinking with,
    224
Insincerity, 114, 213
Inspiration examples, setting, 6
Instincts, being guided by, 153
Intellectual analysis, 195
Internal stress, external demands
    and, 229
Intuition, 183
Intuitive guide, 79–118
  avoiding crisis, 90–92
  calmness and, 105–109
  differences between worry and
    insight, 84–87
  energy flow and, 103–105
  feelings and, 115–118
  hard work and, 99–102
  magic bullet in, 87–90
  making change happen, 95–99
  remaining true, 112–114
  risk taking and, 92–94
  self-labeling and, 109–112
Isolation, environment of, 179

J

James, William, 13–14, 16, 19, 41,
    58, 78, 195, 196, 219
Jobs, Steve, 52
Jones, Jim, 213

Judgment, 54, 63, 117, 132, 166,
    185
Judgmental analysis, 47

K

Kaymer, Martin, 26, 28, 29, 37
Kennedy, Robert, 178
Keys, Tyrone, 179
Kindness, 171, 183
King, Martin Luther, Jr., 119,
    120–121, 178, 195–196,
    208
Kramer, Elizabeth, 69, 86, 90,
    208–209, 214, 215, 218

L

Labeling, outside-in, 48
Lauer, Matt, 59
Leadership
  differences between motivation
    and, 207–211
  true, 215
Lennon, John, 79, 178
"Let It Be," 79–80
Lies, telling, 237
Life
  getting on with, 231
  perceptions of, 234
Life situations, viewing, 228
Lincoln, Abraham, 178, 208, 235
Listening, 213, 214, 231
  to inner wisdom, 4
  to your feelings, 116
Littering, 88
Love
  actions from, 161

encouraging, 159–191

as foundation of inner wisdom, 165

goals and, 161

guiding others to, 209

natural bond between enduring excellence and, 169

relevance of, 189–192

as resilient, secure, and instinctual, 160–161

self-correction to, 158

as simpler than hate, 178

truth of, 227

as universal, 191

M

Mandela, Nelson, 146–147, 208

Manning, Eli, 77

McCartney, Paul, 79

McGonigal, Kelly, 202–203

Medication, 12

Meditation, 95

Mental-conditioning coaches, 12

Mental health

issues of, in sports, 11–12

looking at, through the inside-out, 80

Mental-performance techniques, success and, 3

Mental techniques, 232

Milestones, 65

Mills, Billy, 34–37

Mind

ability to overcome, 4

defined, xi

functioning of the human, 7

intuitive signs of a low state of, 62–66

natural resilience of, 119

principles of, 5, 14

self-corrective power of the, 4, 8, 40, 79, 87, 89–90

time and state of, 71–73

Mindfulness, practicing, 66

Mind-set, 22, 23, 28, 38, 44, 122, 131

calm and quiet, 229

cluttered, 63, 173

contented and clear, 171

ebb and flow of, 38

effect of cluttered, 63

finding optimum, 196

lack of productivity as symptom of inefficient, 129

link between current, and perceptions, 66

subsequent, 234

Mind strategies, myth of, 89

Misdirection of hate, 175–177

Misery, 235

Misinformation, 92

Mood chart, 82, 83–84, 86, 177

Moods, 44,

fluctuation of, 235

low, cure for, 22

Motivation, differences between leadership and, 207–211

Motivational tools, 12

N

National Football League

behavioral policies in, 16–18

Player Protect program of,
16–17, 105
Negativity, 34, 230, 236
concerns on, 232–233
energizing, 28, 64
overcoming, 28, 35, 232–233
replacing, with positive
thoughts, 28–31
Neill, Michael, 89
Nicklaus, Jack, 94
No-resistance path
to a healthy partnership,
172–174
to success, 106–109
Norman, Greg, 51

O

Obama, Barack, 74–75
Obstacles, overcoming, 200–203
Olympic excellence, innate resilience
and, 34–37
Oneness
of life, 177, 178
of success, 177–180
Openness, 183
as foundation of inner wisdom,
165
hidden power of, 165–168
Opportunities, missing, 234
Options, visibility of, 111
Organization, innovative ideas in
waking up, 186–189
Outcomes, self-worth and, 139
Outliers: The Story of Success
(Gladwell), 132
Outlook, constant changes in, 3

Outside events, perception of, 38
Outside-in, 47–48, 67, 76, 78, 201
defined, xii
versus inside-out, 133
self-labeling as, 109
Outside-in labeling, 48
Outside-in mix-up, 174
Outside-in paradigm
fallacy of using, 43
prevalence of the, 147
Out:think Group, 129
Overcome, innate ability to, 6
Overcommunication, 212
Overthinking, 25, 183, 200

P

Palmer, Arnold, 93–94
Panic attacks, 11
Paradigm, 3
defined, xii
grind-it-out, 189
inside-out, 67, 194, 205, 215
outside-in, 43, 147
Parise, Zach, 36–37
Partnership, no-resistance path to
healthy, 172–174
Passion
finding your, 65
source and pursuit, 52–53
Past, 232
illusionary, 69–71
leaving in the past, 188–189
Path of no resistance, 2, 19,
157–158, 215, 221, 223
defined, xii
love and, 240

Peace of mind, and positive
    thinking, 29
Pecking order, creation of, 187
Penn State University, scandal at, 233
Perceptions
    creation of, 33, 45
    of life, 234
    nature of, 1–2
    of the past, 232
    as thought dependent, 69
    varying, 3
Performance
    and positive thinking, 31, 238
    overcoming problems in,
        101–102
    principle of thought and, 19–23
Performance-enhancing drugs,
    56–57
Physical immune system, 3–4
Piccolo, Brian, 204
Pink, Daniel H., 156–157, 202
Player Protect in National Football
    League, 16–17, 105
Positive thinking, 12, 64
    believing in, 30–31
    performance excellence and,
        30, 238
    problems with, 28–31
Potential, innate, 54–56
Pransky, George, 5, 135, 216
Pressure, illusion of experience and,
    49–51
Principles, 9
    defined, xi
The Principles of Psychology (James),
    13

Problem solving, fast track in, 140
Procrastination, 128
Productivity, 237
    lack of, 129
    nature of, 128–131
    reminders in, 130–131
    strategies in, 130–131, 148
Psychological immune system, 3–4,
        78, 125, 152, 207, 217,
        226, 240
    defined, xii
Psychological issues, digging into
        the details of, 14–15
Psychological techniques, 12
Psychology, 15, 218
Psychotic, 80
Pulling back, 121, 128

R
Rage, 117
Reconsideration, power of, 144–146
Relaxation practices, 12
Relevance of love, 189–192
Resilience, 224, 226, 237
    inborn characteristics of, 8
    as innate, 222
    of the mind, 119
Respect, 183
    encouraging, 187
    as foundation of inner wisdom,
        165
    as simpler than hate, 178
Retribution, 155
Risks, taking, 92–94
Robbins, Tony, 201–202
Robinson, Jackie, 178, 235

Rubin, Gretchen, 59
Ruess, Nate, xiii
Rules, 58
   getting handle on, 160
   hours-applied, 135
   limiting, 187
   setting, 150–152, 160
   universal, 159–191
Ryan, Rex, 154

S
Sadness, 235
Salespersons, advice for
      underperforming, 101–102
Sayers, Gale, 204
Self-belief, 36
Self-centered thoughts, not acting
      on, 169
Self-correction, 51, 221
   innate ability for, 4, 138
   keeping at full capacity, 118
   to love, 158
   mind's ability for, 4, 8, 40, 79,
      87, 89–90
Self-help resources, 9, 12
Self-help strategies, 26, 66–68,
      205–206
Self-labeling as self-defeating,
      109–112
Self-worth, 139
   level of, 235
   outcomes and, 139
Sensory experience, thought as source
      of, 73, 167
Shapiro, Mark, 193–195
Showing up, art of, 123–125

Simms, Phil, 77
Simplicity, 70, 218–222
Single-mindedness, 154
Slumps, 100
Smart, Jamie, 128n, 170
Sobel, Jason, 94n
Sports, mental health issues in,
      11–12
Sports psychology, 12, 106
Stale-thinking-out/fresh-thinking-
      in, 207
State of mind, 44
   communication and, 188
   finding answers in, 189
   self-correction of, 8
   time and, 71–73
Staying in the game, 119–158,
      225–226
   art of showing up and, 123–125
   free will and success in,
      146–149
   getting to work, 126–128
   nature of productivity and,
      128–131
   power of reconsidering,
      144–146
   problem-solving fast track,
      140–144
   pursuit of the zone, 135–140
   setting rules, expectations, and
      goals in, 150–158
Steadiness, difference between
      inconsistency and, 94
Steinem, Gloria, 178
Stillpower, 4
   coining of, as term, 123

Stillpower (Kramer), 3–4, 9, 23, 44,
    80–81, 107, 142, 170,
    182
Strasburg, Stephen, 50–51
Strength, sources of, 183
Strength to Love (King), 196n
Stress, 105, 230, 237, 238
Struggles, circumstantial, 227
Success, 155
    calmness and, 105–109
    freedom of, 232
    free will and, 146–149
    hard work as foundation of, 134
    no-resistance path to, 105–109
    oneness of, 177–180
    quest for, 179
    as result of clarity of thought,
        160

T

Talent Is Overrated (Colvin),
    132–134
Teresa, Mother, 178, 208
Thinking. See Thought(s)
Thought(s)
    bound-up, 173, 169
    controlling, 202–203, 224, 232,
        239
    defined, xi
    disconcerted, 196
    distrusting, 18, 225
    dysfunctional, 32, 81, 97, 117
    errant, 16, 28, 75
    ever-changing nature of, 199
    fearful, 27
    free-flowing, 27

implications of understanding,
    37–41
judgmental, 182
manipulating, 31
mismanagement of, 6
neutrality of, 228
noticing your, 28
obstacles, figments of, 228
principles of, 14, 179–180
    innate, 5
lesson from Hurricane Sandy
    on, 181–183
performance and, 19–23
randomness of, 228
revved-up, 137
secret lies in, 23–25
self-centered, 169
as source of sensory experiences,
    73, 167
struggles from, 227
success as result of clarity of,
    160
tie to circumstances, 20–21
troubling, 23
Thought-feeling connection, 6, 8,
    15, 38, 61, 74, 85, 87, 90,
    95, 118, 209
    as building block of human
        experience, 115
    defined, xii
    relevance of, 128
    understanding, 115–116,
        162–163
Time, passage of, in erasing hurt,
    119–120
Time management, 47–48

Time-out, taking a, 157
Titmuss, Richard, 156
Togetherness, as simpler than hate, 178
Tolle, Eckhart, 66
True, remaining, 112–114
Truth, in effective communication, 211–214

U
Uncertainty, feeling of, 124
Understanding, 183
    versus application, 203–207, 229
    as foundation of inner wisdom, 165
    hidden power of, 165–169
Universal rule, 159–191

V
Venegas, Maria, 81–83, 84, 86, 107, 177
Visentin, Deb, 142–144

W
Weight loss, 46, 96
Willpower, 76
    success and, 3
The Willpower Instinct (McGonigal), 202–203

Winfrey, Oprah, 66, 170–171
Winning, 186, 235
Wisdom
    as everywhere, 79
    imparting, 135
    love, compassion, understanding, respect, and openness as foundation of inner, 165
    unfolding from inside, 165
Woods, Tiger, 131–134
Woolf, Gina, 216
Work. See also Hard work
    getting to, 126–128
World of form, 44–46, 49
Worry, differences between insight and, 84–87

Y
You Can Be Happy No Matter What (Carlson), 197
Yourself, believing in, 200

Z
Zone, 73, 135–141
    pursuit of the, 135–140, 158, 230

ABOUT THE AUTHOR

Garret Kramer is also the author of *Stillpower* and the founder of Inner Sports. His inside-out approach to performance excellence has transformed the way players, coaches, professional teams, and parents view the athletic experience. A consultant, speaker, and columnist, Kramer has been featured in *Sports Illustrated*, *Forbes*, the *New York Times*, and the *Wall Street Journal*. He lives in New Vernon, New Jersey, with his family. The author invites readers to e-mail him at gkramer@innersports.com.

ABOUT INNER SPORTS

Inner Sports is a mental-performance and consulting practice located in Morristown, New Jersey. Founded as a boutique sports psychology firm by Garret Kramer in 1995, Inner Sports's client list has grown to include athletes, coaches, agents, and management executives throughout professional and collegiate sports. Inner Sports also conducts seminars, workshops, and lectures for corporations, businesses, and schools. The guiding principle behind the success of Inner Sports is simple: The ability to overcome is innate. Looking outside for answers only inhibits one's free will, instincts, productivity, and happiness. You can contact Inner Sports at info@innersports.com.